HELP YOUR PARTNER SAY 'YES'

Seven steps to achieving
better cooperation and
communication

ANDREW G. MARSHALL

BLOOMSBURY
LONDON · BERLIN · NEW YORK · SYDNEY

To Rebecca Alexander

Thank you for the inspiration.

First published in Great Britain 2011

Copyright © 2011 by Andrew G. Marshall

The moral right of the author has been asserted

Bloomsbury Publishing Plc
36 Soho Square
London W1D 3QY

Bloomsbury Publishing, London, New York and Berlin

ISBN 978 1 4088 0263 2

10 9 8 7 6 5 4 3 2 1

Typeset by Hewer Text UK Ltd, Edinburgh
Printed in Great Britain by Clays Limited, St Ives Plc

MIX
Paper from
responsible sources
FSC® C018072

www.bloomsbury.com/andrewgmarshall

Seven steps to achieving better cooperation and communication

INTRODUCTION

Help Your Partner Say 'Yes' is part of a series of books offering straightforward advice for creating successful and fulfilling relationships. Getting the most out of love needs skills and the good news is that these skills can be learned. Nowhere is this more important than when you're trying to get your partner to cooperate in some cherished plan or in making day-to-day living run more smoothly.

If you've picked up this book, you are probably frustrated about not being able to get through to your partner; maybe small issues about running the house have begun to accumulate, or perhaps your relationship is in crisis and you're trying to persuade your partner to give it another try. Whatever the circumstances, this book will help you step back, understand why you're making little or no progress, and learn alternative strategies which will enable you to persuade, rather than cajole, beg, manipulate or nag, your partner.

In devising this programme, I have drawn on the latest research about persuasion and twenty-five years' experience working as a marital therapist. However, I have changed names and details, and sometimes merged two or three of my clients' stories to protect their identity and confidentiality. In addition, I have used interviews with people not in counselling and letters written to my website. My thanks to everyone who has shared their experiences and made this book possible.

Andrew G. Marshall
www.andrewgmarshall.com

STEP 1

STOP WHAT DOESN'T WORK

Wouldn't it be wonderful if you could just ask nicely and your partner would go along with your request? Wouldn't life be much simpler if the two of you could agree the best course of action and get on with it rather than getting bogged down in arguments, stonewalling or procrastination? If this sounds like an impossible dream, don't worry, because my seven-step programme will help you identify the sticking points, communicate more effectively and change your relationship for the better. In a nutshell, you will learn how to persuade your partner to say 'yes'.

But first, it is important to stress that my programme is not about manipulating or hoodwinking your partner, but about putting your thoughts across clearly and ensuring that your message is heard. I will also teach you how to read your partner better and build trust, so that he or she is favourably disposed to your suggestions. In many ways, the art of persuasion is as much about changing the way you come across as changing your partner. In fact, as the book progresses, you will discover your behaviour and that of your partner are inextricably linked.

Up to now, you have probably tried a variety of ways to get your partner to change, but with little success. Common sense would suggest that, if they haven't worked, you should stop and try something else. Unfortunately, most people keep on with the same, failed strategy, in the hope that doing it bigger, louder or just one more time will provide the breakthrough. Sadly, they just dig themselves into a bigger hole.

So the first step is to stop digging and throw away the spade.

Seven Failed Strategies

None of these strategies is particularly effective – beyond the short term – but we keep on plugging away regardless. Which of the following have you used?

Lecturing

Definition: Assuming the position of an expert or all-seeing prophet (who can foresee all the pitfalls) and telling your partner the errors of his or her ways – over and over again.

In action: 'I wouldn't do it like that' or 'You're not going to . . .?' Although someone who lectures might think that they are being helpful, they really want to control their partner and ensure he or she performs the task their way.

'My wife believes there is only one way to change a nappy – with at least three baby wipes pulled out in advance and wiping down rather than up – and she has a real go if I don't follow her instructions to the letter,' explained Richard. At the same time, his wife, Caroline, would complain that he didn't help enough with the baby. 'But you don't want help, you want staff to order about,' Richard countered.

How it backfires: Assuming that you know best invites rebellion either overtly or covertly.

What's the alternative? Offer help and then step back; your partner will either learn from his or her mistakes or return and ask for advice. Richard soon discovered that some of his wife's instructions were helpful and that if, for example, he didn't fasten the straps properly, the nappy would sag. Caroline discovered she was much more relaxed and able to enjoy family time together, if she wasn't monitoring the amount of baby powder Richard used.

Sarcasm

Definition: Using mocking or contemptuous put-downs which are designed to control by making the other person feel small or stupid.

In action: This strategy goes hand in hand with sniping (hidden or sly undermining) and snapping with impatience. When Martin brought home an espresso coffee machine that one of his mates had bought but changed his mind about, he was upset that Kimberly didn't seem very grateful: 'She was doing stuff online and beyond a cursory look didn't come down to give me a hand setting up the machine. It took some of the shine off the surprise – and she's the coffee drinker not me.' So Martin shouted up the stairs: 'If it's not too much trouble, could you come down and try this?'

How it backfires: Nobody likes criticism and most people fight back with similar ammunition. Indeed Kimberly sniped back: 'The milk isn't very frothy. Did you read the instructions?'

What's the alternative? However strong the temptation to respond to your partner's barbed comments, don't rise to the bait – but simply walk away. When your temper is more under control, explain how you feel and discuss the issues with your partner. When Martin and Kimberly both calmed down – after rowing all evening – Martin explained how he'd been looking forward to her reaction and Kimberly apologised.

Demanding

Definition: Issuing commands rather than requests. Someone using this strategy does not expect to be told 'no' or to be contradicted.

In action: This normally happens when someone feels they are in the right and therefore that their partner is in the wrong (even though life is seldom this black and white). When Siobhan discovered that her husband, Declan, had had an affair, she demanded that he take her away for a second honeymoon: 'You've spent enough on that woman, you can spend a little on me.' However, she was so busy imposing her will on Declan that she was unable to hear his concerns: 'How is going away going to change things between us?' Rather than answering his question, Siobhan just restated her case but this time with tears: 'He's broken my heart but he won't even do this little thing for me.'

How it backfires: Although people may give in to demands, they subvert in sneaky ways, like finding millions of excuses for never quite getting round to the task. Alternatively, like Declan, they just dig their heels in and refuse to budge – even an inch – fearing that their partner will steamroller them into submission.

What's the alternative? Negotiating. In this way, your partner is allowed to express his or her opinions (which may or may not be valid), discuss the timescale for a project, and take joint ownership of it. When Declan and Siobhan finished counselling and resolved the underlying problems in their marriage, they did indeed choose and plan a weekend away together.

Nagging

Definition: The first time is asking, the second time reminding, but further repetition becomes nagging.

In action: Nothing polarises a couple more quickly than nagging. The person being nagged feels their partner is always finding fault (and therefore feels hard done by), while the person nagging – and it's something of which both men and women are guilty – feels powerless and angry.

'If she doesn't like being nagged, she could put her shoes away,' says James, twenty-eight, 'but she kicks them off and leaves them for me to trip over. I've tried asking, I've tried explaining that I could easily damage them, I've tried throwing them over her side of the bedroom. I'll talk until I'm blue in the face and, although she might remember for a few days, nothing really changes.' Although James thought he'd been trying lots of different ways of communicating, he'd actually just been nagging. Unfortunately, his girlfriend, Michelle, just switched off. Worse still, she used his 'unreasonable' nagging to justify carrying on as before.

How it backfires: Nobody likes to nag and nobody likes to be nagged. It creates a slow poison that seeps through a relationship.

What's the alternative? Bring all the hostility up to the surface by asking: 'How can we resolve this problem?' Be prepared to listen to your partner's viewpoint and this will encourage him or her to listen to yours. James explained that he felt taken for granted – and not appreciated for what he did around the house – and Michelle explained what it felt like to be hounded. They were finally ready to cooperate.

Inducing guilt

Definition: Manipulating a partner by making him or her feel responsible for your upset or by convincing them that they have committed an offence.

In action: It normally starts with a prod to get sympathy or pity: 'I never see my children' or 'my life is a mess', and if someone else has a bad day, it's 'not as bad as mine' – but really this strategy is a request for a free pass to get your own way. The next step up reminds your partner how much he or she is in debt: 'After everything I've done for you' or 'I don't like washing your games kit'. However, there is a more sinister twist.

'My girlfriend and I were at the supermarket and I ran into an old friend who is almost like a sister to me,' explains Jake, twenty-nine. 'She helped me through a bad patch and I did a lot of baby-sitting for her when her husband left. I hadn't seen her for a while so I stopped and chatted. I could tell my girlfriend was getting more and more annoyed, so I made my apologies and got on with the shopping. Immediately, my girlfriend started having a go about how inconsiderate I'd been and how I'd ignored her – even though I'd introduced her and tried to involve her in our conversation. I was "disrespectful". I "didn't consider her feelings". I "had no boundaries". To be honest, I didn't really understand, but I apologised for upsetting her – except that it didn't make any difference. She was in such a mood that she drove out of the supermarket without looking and almost crashed into another car – and that was my fault too.' In effect, Jake's girlfriend was taking a minor or imaginary offence, winding herself up over it and then blaming Jake for upsetting her.

How it backfires: Although this strategy will often get the desired effect, any victory feels hollow, as nothing is freely given by their partner, and the guilt inducer, who already suffers from low self-esteem, feels even more worthless.

What's the alternative? Instead of blaming your partner, and therefore giving him or her all the power to remedy the situation, look at your own part in the problem. Not only is it easier to change your behaviour than to force change on to your partner but also taking control is empowering.

Placating

Definition: Trying to appease, sweet-talk and pacify your partner and thereby take the edge off his or her bad mood.

In action: Martha and Greg had been married for fifteen years, but for much of that time Greg had suffered from depression. 'Obviously, I've tried to be supportive and understanding,' said Martha, 'but sometimes I think I've spent my whole life tiptoeing round him, monitoring his mood and trying to keep everything nice. I know I want to grow old with him, but not this gloomy, insecure, sleeping-all-weekend version of him. But I don't say any of this because I'm worried about making him feel worse.' Unfortunately, she had built up a head of resentment: 'What about me? It would be good not to be taken for granted.'

How it backfires: Whether you are using smiles (that are put on), too-ready agreement or forced humour, you are still trying to control. Worse still, this strategy often makes the other person even more annoyed.

What's the alternative? It is much better to address the issues – however unpleasant – rather than side-step a row.

Dropping hints

Definition: Hoping your partner will guess or know what is needed, rather than asking outright for it.

In action: Sometimes this strategy can be quite aggressive – 'If you loved me, you'd know' – but generally it comes from a position of weakness. Certainly Martha didn't expect anyone to be interested in her needs, so even if she felt down and wanted a hug, she wouldn't say anything: 'I've always got my satisfaction from looking after other people; the children and Greg have always come first.'

'What would happen if you did ask?' I enquired.

Martha was silent for a while. 'If you don't really ask, then you don't have to deal with the rejection when you don't get.'

How it backfires: Clues can be misinterpreted and hints can be so subtle that they are missed altogether.

What's the alternative? Value yourself and accept that it is OK to have needs and to express them.

WHY DO I ADOPT THIS STRATEGY?

One of the best ways of breaking out of unhelpful behaviour is by identifying why you do it.

1. **Understand the roots.** Our first experiences of being persuasive come when we are only two or three years old. Our language skills are not very well developed and we are too young to understand concepts such as negotiation or compromise. Worse still, our parents hold all the cards. It is not surprising that as children we learn to wheedle, demand or throw

tantrums. In many ways, the seven failed strategies are more sophisticated versions of toddler behaviour.

2. **Understand the patterns.** We discover how relationships work from watching our parents and siblings interact. How would your mother get her way? How would your father impose his will? What would your brothers and sisters do? Who was in charge? How did they maintain their top-dog status? What are the links between how your family behaved and how you try to influence your partner?

3. **Understand the danger points.** Look back at the last three times you had a row or were left frustrated at not being able to influence your partner's behaviour. What were the common themes? Were you tired or stressed? Had problems from work seeped into your personal life? Were you feeling unappreciated and therefore particularly vulnerable? By knowing the signs, you can be extra vigilant next time and think twice before behaving in the same old way.

The Three Keys to Successful Persuasion

Once you have stopped wasting energy and good-will on strategies that don't work, there is space to look at what does.

Equality

The failed strategies have one thing in common: a power imbalance. In the first three, the more powerful partner tries to bludgeon the other into submission and in the last three, the less power-ful partner tries to manipulate the more powerful one. (With nagging, there is a twisted version of equality as two matched partners try to force and resist each other.) So what's the alternative? In true equality, as opposed to nagging, there is a benefit for each partner from the solution. Sometimes each partner has separate spheres of control – for example, one will be in charge of money, the other in charge of their social life – but each will consult the other and major decisions are made jointly. All in all, each partner will control about 50 per cent of their life together.

Martin and Kimberly, whom we met earlier in the chapter, arrived into counselling in crisis.

Their fights were so destructive that even a minor disagreement would spiral out of control and ruin their whole week.

A typical example was when Martin came home and found Kimberly cleaning the saucepan they used to cook their pet ferrets' food. 'She was about to tip the soapy water all over the garden. I asked her to stop because it would ruin the plants,' said Martin, 'but she just looked at me and poured it anyway.' He had hardly finished explaining when Kimberly jumped in: 'You didn't ask, you shouted. If you'd stopped and asked, I'd have told you that it wasn't soapy water but the last rinse.' Martin gave her a black look and went straight back on the attack: 'So why not put it down the drain?' Kimberly was so angry that I thought she was about to walk out of my counselling room: 'How could I with all your junk lying around?' They both felt the problem was the other's unreasonable behaviour and if only he or she would change, everything would be fine.

When we looked back at this argument, towards the end of their counselling, they were not only able to laugh, but were also able to identify that the breakthrough had been when both of them started changing – equally. 'When I didn't lose my temper, Martin didn't close in on himself and shut me out,' said Kimberly. 'When I didn't retreat and keep my feelings and thoughts to myself, Kimberly stopped blowing her top,' said Martin.

Putting yourself in your partner's shoes

From where we stand, our solution makes complete sense. We understand the thought process that helped us reach this conclusion. If our preferred option seems a little one-sided, there is a good reason or a good excuse. Meanwhile, our partner has been through a parallel process – but while we expect him or her to listen to us, we are not quite so ready to offer the same courtesy. All too often, we half listen, throw in a bit of our own interpretation, and jump to the wrong conclusion. So while we put our actions down to the *best* possible motives, we can easily put our partner's down to the *worst* ones. But what would happen if you understood your partner's position as well as your own?

When Martin and Kimberly stopped countering each other's arguments and started listening or asking for further explanation, they began to understand each other better. 'We both come from families where nobody listened to us,' said Kimberly. 'And now, instead of making assumptions – often the wrong ones – we've started to check it out first,' added Martin.

Win/Win solutions

When you and your partner see each other as adversaries, the goal is outright victory or to win concessions. Therefore, the strategy becomes to dig in to your position, mislead or use tricks to get your own way. The result is either a Win/Lose situation where only one side sees the outcome as positive (and the other is less likely to accept the solution voluntarily) or a Lose/Lose situation where both parties end up worse off.

The alternative is a Win/Win solution where both parties benefit and therefore the solutions stick. So how do you achieve this goal? The secret is to understand that behind every bargaining position there are not only needs and desires but also concerns and fears too. Our natural inclination is to close down debate, as we fear that the more competing interests come to the surface, the harder it will be to find a solution. However, Win/Win depends on identifying as many interests as possible. In fact, the more we know about both our own true needs and those of our partner, the easier it becomes to find a solution that benefits everyone.

With the focus on interests – rather than positions – and by considering multiple criteria rather than looking for one answer, we can begin to use reason and yield to principles rather than pressure. This process not only reduces our fears but also, once all the needs are in the open, it is easier to help each other. Before too long, we have become a team, rather than adversaries, and a Win/Win solution is almost inevitable. So how does it work in practice?

When Martin and Kimberly discussed their finances – each had a separate bank account – they shared their needs, desires, concerns and fears. Their need was to find a simpler way to run their household accounts rather than forever debating whose turn it was to pay. Kimberly desired a joint account, so that she wouldn't feel like a small girl asking Daddy for money. Martin's concern was that the bills got paid on time. 'I'm not frightened that she will blow the budget – although I've had girlfriends before who were hopeless with money – because she's really quite good with finances,' he said. 'Actually, my job involves keeping an eye on costs,' Kimberly added. So they decided to keep their individual accounts but to set up a joint one for household bills. It was a classic Win/Win solution. Kimberly became more involved in their finances; Martin had some of the pressure of balancing the budget taken off him.

TURN IT ROUND

Next time a contentious issue comes up between you and your partner, put it to this test:

- **Do I really want it?** Sometimes being denied something or your partner telling you what to do can put your back up and launch a fight. Instead of acting on automatic pilot, stop and check whether this is something you truly want rather than something you just think you want.
- **Is it really fair?** What would an independent arbitrator say? Do you have a reasonable case? If you strip away all your self-justifications – probably drawn from a different part of your life – how fair is this particular request?
- **Is it really important?** Lots of bitter arguments are over matters of principle rather than over a particular issue. When the matters of principle are removed, arguments like Martin and Kimberly's over how to clean the ferrets' saucepan are neither that contentious nor worth the amount of upset caused.
- **Think past the moment.** Although using one of your old strategies to win an advantage might feel good, think past your moment of triumph to the mood in the house over the next few days and then on to the impact on your relationship.

Summing Up

We think that we've used a variety of strategies to gain our partner's cooperation but really we've used the same failed ones over and over again. These include lecturing, sarcasm, demanding (trying to be more powerful than your partner), inducing guilt, placating and dropping hints (imagining your partner has all the power). The other strategy is nagging, which sets up a classic Lose/Lose situation where nothing is achieved and both parties feel powerless. The alternative is to place yourself in your partner's shoes, look for solutions that are equal and allow both of you to win.

IN A NUTSHELL:
- When you stop trying to force change, your partner will stop resisting change.
- Goodwill can return to your relationship.
- Your partner is finally open to being persuaded.

STEP 2

DO LESS

Whenever long-married couples are asked the secret of their success, they invariably reply: you have to work at things. But shouldn't our relationships be a source of joy rather than something to knuckle down under? The other problem with working on a relationship is that it suggests making big changes – such as setting up a weekly 'date' night, going on a second honeymoon or making big sacrifices (for example, giving up a friend whom your partner dislikes or cutting back on a hobby that eats into family time). Twenty-five years' experience as a marital therapist has shown me that these big changes seldom deliver the big benefits that couples desire. Date night might work a few times but problems getting babysitters soon undermine good intentions, the glow of the second honeymoon quickly wears off, and people soon resent their sacrifices. Worse still, when the big effort changes very little, couples begin to believe their relationship is doomed.

So if 'working' on your relationship can so easily backfire, what about the other extreme: doing nothing? With this strategy, however, there's a real danger of slipping into taking each other for granted, and nobody wants that either.

Fortunately, there is an alternative to these extremes: the middle way.

The Lazy Guide to Working on Your Relationship

All the ideas given below are fun, simple and don't take much effort. However, taken together, they can overhaul your relationship and turn time together from dull into desirable.

Spend ten minutes chatting over your day

Instead of big dramatic gestures – which are hard to repeat – try to set up good relationship habits. The most important one is checking in with each other when you return home – instead of, for example, starting supper or checking emails.

A few moments sharing the highs and the lows of the day prevents misunderstandings – such as believing your partner's bad mood is down to you rather than his or her demanding boss – which can ruin a whole evening together. The more details in your daily chat, the more involved you become in each other's triumphs and disasters. Some couples find it hard to share – after years of broad brush-strokes of 'fine' or 'same old thing'. So remember small anecdotes and snippets of gossip about friends and save them up for the evening. A good tip is to sit down and eat together – without the television on – as this gives enough time together for the natural rhythms of conversation to kick in.

Watch each other's favourite television show

Instead of catching up on chores, watching another channel in a different room, or going online, commit to sitting through each other's must-see show. This will provide something new to discuss and demonstrate that you are truly interested in each other – even the inconvenient bits, such as an obsession with axle grease or a passion for fashion. What's more, we have a real animal need to be close to another human being, and snuggling up together on the sofa is not only a good way to unwind but also shows that you can be intimate without it necessarily leading to sex.

Kiss with your eyes open

Actually looking at each other when you kiss is incredibly intimate and can also be the gateway to more erotic lovemaking. Perhaps that's why this is the most controversial of my ideas. Some couples find the idea silly or feel uncomfortable looking at each other. They believe it is more 'romantic' to keep their eyes closed, but this makes us concentrate on the sensation rather than the person.

When couples arrive in my office with one partner complaining 'You're not the person I thought you were', I can almost guarantee that they have been kissing with their eyes closed and getting lost in their own fantasies. So persevere, overcome the awkwardness, and become more aware of both your partner and yourself and take lovemaking to a whole new level.

Another associated idea is to mix up your kissing style: try butterfly kisses (very light and not just on the mouth but all over your partner's face), nibbling kisses (gentle bites on the lips or other sensual areas like the ears), or breathy, languid kisses, tasting and smelling each other's body.

Buy something small but fun

It could be her favourite bar of chocolate or a novelty key ring for him, but a present shows that you're thinking about your partner even when apart. Unlike birthdays and Christmas, when it is tempting to buy presents your partner 'needs' – such as clothes you think make her look sexy or tools for jobs you'd like him to do around the house – these gifts are pure fun or indulgence. There is a second advantage: by demonstrating the sort of spontaneous appreciation that you'd like – where flowers are not just for birthdays but 'because I saw these and thought of you' and saying 'thank you' is not just for completing major projects but everyday chores too – you are encouraging your partner to adopt the same behaviour.

Share a bath

There are few better ways of unwinding after a long, hard day than by having a soak in the bath, but instead of making it a solitary pursuit, invite your partner along. I counselled one couple who bathed together every day – as somewhere to talk without the kids interrupting. A twist on this idea, which is always popular with my clients, is to bring along a large bowl of ice cream and one spoon. It is very sensual to feed each other something cold in a hot bath. Sharing a bath, and washing each other's hair, will also help you and your partner to feel comfortable being naked together and it improves overall intimacy.

Go to bed at the same time or enjoy a lie-in together

If you and your partner's body clocks are on different time zones, and you're seldom awake in bed together, the chances of making love are close to zero. So make a conscious choice to communicate better over bedtimes. Instead of saying, 'I'm going up now' and hoping that your partner will follow, invite him or her. Instead of watching any old rubbish on television until you're tired enough to sleep, come upstairs for a cuddle and drift off in each other's arms. Skip jobs such as loading the washing machine or checking emails before going upstairs, or you'll miss the window when your partner is still awake. If you have radically different bedtimes, try finding a compromise where, for example, your partner goes up a little earlier and you stay up a little longer, and meet in the middle. Conversely, give yourself a treat, let the children look after themselves next Sunday morning, and enjoy a lie-in together.

Give in with good grace

Living with someone inevitably means having to compromise and do things that you'd rather not do. Next time you have to attend her miserable work do or hold a piece of wood that he's sawing through, don't just grit your teeth, but look for the hidden pleasures. Even if you have to 'act as if' you're enjoying yourself, after a while you will probably start to believe it. Not only will your partner be grateful but he or she will also go the extra mile for you in return.

Look at each other more

When they're talking, couples in love spend 75 per cent of their time looking at each other. Most settled couples are too busy buttoning up their children's coats or buttering sandwiches to make eye contact – even when communicating something important. In fact, they only look at each other for 30 to 60 per cent of the time and therefore miss the subtleties of body language and misinterpret each other's tone of voice.

While good eye contact makes you seem attentive and sincere, poor eye contact makes your partner think you are talking *at* them rather than to them. So at the very least, make a commitment to be in the same room rather than shouting up the stairs.

Report your negative feelings rather than show them

In modern Britain, we are forever being told to express our feelings. But, when it comes to anger, getting things off your chest can often pump up your emotions rather than reduce them. Worse still, having a rant will either encourage your partner to fight back – and escalate matters further – or to sulk, switch off or walk away (which means nothing gets sorted). So instead of showing your feelings, try reporting them. By this I mean: 'I felt angry when you didn't answer me' or 'I was disappointed when you were late', rather than snapping, sniping or shouting. Your partner will probably apologise or offer an explanation and the two of you can have a civilised discussion about how to do things differently.

Echo each other

This is the simplest and most effective way of improving communication. When your partner has finished telling you something, repeat back the last thing said. For example: 'So you just stood there.' This might seem weird, but it shows your partner that he or she has your full attention. It also encourages him or her to open up and tell you more. The final benefit of echoing back is that it takes the pressure off you to think up a searching question. Although this strategy might feel a little artificial at first, persevere and it will soon become second nature. There is more advice about improving communication in the next exercise.

HOW GOOD A LISTENER ARE YOU?

The best way of influencing someone is to understand their thought processes and their line of reasoning. To achieve this goal, we imagine that we need to ask clever or searching questions, but the truth is our partner is telling us all we need to know in their everyday conversation. The problem is that much of the time we're not listening. The following quiz tests if you are a good listener or not:

1. When your partner is having trouble finding the words to express themselves, what are you most likely to do?
   a) Finish off his or her sentence.
   b) Nod encouragingly.

2. When your partner needs help with a problem at work, what is most likely to happen?
   a) I will offer advice or come up with a way forward.
   b) I will ask for more information, so that I really understand the situation and check that all possible avenues are explored.

3. How often does your partner complain that you interrupt?
   a) Quite often, he or she will say, 'If you'll just let me finish'.
   b) We generally hear each other out.

4. When your partner is recounting a story about something that happened during the day, which of the following are you most likely to be doing?
   a) Going through a difficult problem at work, keeping an eye on the children, or ticking off which jobs have been done and which have yet to be done.

    b) Picturing what your partner is talking about or making encouraging noises like 'yes', 'really' or 'tell me more'.

5. When your partner is moaning or complaining about something you've done, what are you thinking about?
    a) Ways to refute the complaint or about his or her equally irritating failings.
    b) Does he or she have a fair case?

6. Which of the following do you naturally prefer?
    a) Talking.
    b) Listening.

Mostly a)

Although you hear what is being said to you – and can repeat chunks of information back – you are not really listening. There are probably tapes playing in your brain and other forms of intrusive thinking that are stopping you from paying your partner the level of attention that you'd like yourself. Next time your mind wanders mentally push the thought out of your head – you can attend to it later – and concentrate on what is being said.

Mostly b)

Congratulations. You are a good listener. However, look back at the areas where you answered a) rather than b). Actively listening – i.e., asking questions and really trying to understand your partner without jumping to conclusions – is really difficult. How could you improve?

Think Small

Change is unsettling. It makes us anxious and frightened. Worse still, we are programmed to respond to fear in one of two ways: fight or flight. But don't worry, there's a way round this problem. It's called Kaizen, from the Japanese for 'change' (kai) and 'good' (zen), and stresses the importance of continuous improvement. Instead of trying for big changes, Kaizen aims to bypass our fears and our natural inclination to stick with the familiar by taking small steps.

In a famous study, Southern Californian householders were asked to put up a small 'Be a safe driver' sign in their windows. Most people agreed to do so. Two weeks later, the team returned and this time asked the volunteers to put up a huge sign – bearing the same message – on their front lawns. They were shown pictures, so there could be no mistake that these signs would dwarf their homes. To make the billboards even less attractive, the lettering was poorly executed. At the same time, the team visited another neighbourhood, which matched the profile of the first but where the residents had not previously agreed to take the small sign. Not surprisingly, only 17 per cent of these householders agreed to display the safe driver billboard. In contrast, 76 per cent of the homes with a small sign opted for the large sign. The small step had made them four times as likely to take the big step.

When couples are stuck and unable to find a way forward, I find Kaizen can break the deadlock. This is how it can work for you:

Ask small questions

Our brain actually likes small questions; this is why we do quizzes and puzzles or enjoy explaining to friends the best way to cook a ham. We feel good when we know the answer and, with little at stake, don't feel a fool if we get something wrong.

Jane and Christopher, in their late thirties, had a big problem. He was fed up with his work, bored with everyday life, and felt that all the passion had drained out of their relationship: 'We have nothing whatsoever in common. When I have free time, I'd much rather be out shooting with the dogs than at home with Jane. Surely, that's wrong.' He hadn't quite gone as far as saying he didn't love her any more but Jane worried that their relationship had no future. 'I wish I hadn't told you and had just pretended that everything was OK,' said Christopher. Jane countered: 'What good is that going to do? We've got to get this sorted. I can't hang around waiting for you to decide if you want me or not.' Before arriving in counselling, they had used only big solutions and Jane had asked Christopher to sleep at his parents' for a week.

'What did that achieve, beyond making me get up earlier and get even more tired?' he complained.

'I thought it would give you space to think,' said Jane.

'By the time we'd put the children to bed and I'd driven round to their house, I had enough time to make a cup of tea and go to bed.'

Using the Kaizen way, I didn't ask big questions like: Why do you feel this way? (As Christopher probably would have answered: 'I don't know. If I knew, do you think I'd be putting myself through all this?') Instead, I asked the couple to consider: 'What small step could you take towards improving your relationship?' and 'What one special thing about you and your partner could you build on?'

Breakthrough tip: Frame your question as a positive. Instead of 'Why don't you fancy me?' turn it into 'How could we improve our sex life?'

Solve small problems

Many people find it hard to think of any small problems in their relationship, especially when the large ones are staring them in the face. However, it is just these minor irritations that slowly undermine a relationship. By ignoring small problems – because we're too busy with day-to-day life or it doesn't seem worth rocking the boat – we redefine them as 'normal' and lose sight of them altogether.

So if you're unable to come up with any small problems, close your eyes and picture what happens on a normal day between you and your partner – moment by moment. Start with getting up in the morning and end with going to bed. Every time there is something that makes you wince – however small – stop your imaginary movie and write down the 'normal' problem.

Before too long, you will have a list of small issues to consider.

When Jane did this exercise, during a solo session, she stopped in the middle of describing preparing breakfast for the children. (Christopher had a long commute but would get up at the last minute and hardly have enough time to drink a mug of coffee.) 'From time to time, he'll complain that I haven't put on the coffee machine and he's got to drink instant, but he doesn't understand that Lola is a fussy eater and Jack won't sit at the table. I've got my hands full. If he cares that much, he should get up five minutes earlier.'

'What message does that give Christopher?' I asked.

Jane thought for a while. 'That I put the children first.'

A small problem – making coffee in the morning – had been categorised as 'normal' and therefore ignored. So instead of trying to deal with big issues – such as bringing the passion back into their relationship – Jane made a pot of fresh coffee in the morning. At their next joint session, their mood had lightened. We still had a long way to go but the sense of stuckness – that nothing could ever change – had gone.

Breakthrough tip: Be as specific as possible about the problem. Don't go for global issues such as 'Show some respect' or 'Help more around the house', but make them specific: 'Don't interrupt me when I'm trying to tell you something' or 'Transfer the clothes from the washing machine to the drier when you get home.'

Take small steps

Small questions throw the spotlight on small problems which need to be solved by small steps. It is also helpful if you can find something that comes up fairly often, so that you can check your progress. Kaizen also works best when the solutions can be implemented straight away.

As their counselling progressed, Jane began to agree with Christopher's diagnosis of their relationship: 'He's right. We don't do enough together. Before the kids were born, when we were courting, I'd go off with him and the dog on their shooting expeditions, but after a while there seemed better things to do.' So she decided to ask her mother to take the children one Sunday and, as an experiment, go with Christopher to one of his club shoots. 'I told myself to have an open mind – because it can be cold and boring – but I found myself really enjoying it. There had been a light dusting of snow and the countryside looked wonderful. I was out in the fresh air and it was really nice watching how Christopher and the dog worked as a team. There were other wives to talk to and we had lunch in a pub with an open fire.'

Christopher was equally pleased: 'It was great to be able to share with you.'

'And you touched my knee – by the fire.'

'It felt right.'

Jane was not going to attend every shoot but they had taken a small step in the right direction.

Breakthrough tip: Double-check that the changes are truly small. If your goal is, for example, to improve your diet, giving up chocolate might seem a small step but actually it could be hard to follow through. However, if your small step is to throw away the first square of every bar, this would be reasonably easy. Over the coming weeks, you could throw away more and more chocolate. Next, you could leave half of your dessert in a restaurant and so on.

The Kaizen way stresses that it is better to build on small success than make a big gesture that is likely to fail. If you're looking for inspiration for a small step to change your relationship, try the following exercise:

REMEMBERING THE MAGIC
OF THE FIRST MEETING

For five years, I did a series of magazine profiles of celebrities and their partners. I would always start by asking for the story of how the couple first met. Within seconds the atmosphere in the room would change – any nerves or apprehension would disappear – and I would feel real warmth as people remembered. The secret is in the detail I asked for: Where were you? What were you wearing? What did you eat? What did your partner look like? What did she say? What did he do? Normally, people have boiled their 'how we met' story into one or two sentences but this reflex story does not provide enough material to trigger proper memories. Over and over again, the celebrities – normally on tight time schedules – would stretch the time allocated for my interview. I was taking them back to the magic of their first meeting and everybody enjoyed lingering on these passionate memories a while longer.

Either write a short story about your memories of how you met your partner or bring the topic up in general conversation – perhaps over a meal. It normally takes three or four questions to get someone in the mood. To give you an idea, here is the first part of my interview with Twiggy and her husband, Leigh Lawson (an actor best known for his role as Alec D'Urberville in Polanski's film *Tess*). See how many facts I extracted:

Twiggy started: 'In 1985, I went out for dinner at Caprice in London with three friends. At another table I spotted Jonathan Pryce – whom I'd been working with – so I went over to say hello. Immediately this handsome man stood up. It was Leigh, who reminded me that we'd met ten years earlier at a John Denver concert. Even back then I'd thought him really dishy, but we'd both been married then so nothing romantic crossed my mind. This time the chemistry must have been obvious because I remember telling my friends to stop trying to pair me off. But I must have been curious because I bought a magazine with a big interview with Leigh. I learned he had been alone for two years and after the trauma of the break-up was not interested in seeing anyone seriously for the next ten years! Three days later Robert Powell and his wife, Babs, who used to be in Pan's People, invited me to a restaurant in Chelsea. By a string of amazing coincidences, Leigh was invited too. We chatted and laughed but on paper he was trouble. Who in their right mind would trust a gorgeous actor? I was no longer an eighteen-year-old about to jump in head first. So I let him slip away again. Fate had other ideas.'

At this point, Leigh takes up the story: 'I thought Twiggy was absolutely gorgeous – but as she was one of the most beautiful women in the world I knew everybody would be after her phone number. Despite fate throwing the two of us into the same restaurant twice in one week, I said good night and let her walk away. Perhaps I lacked confidence; perhaps my heart had just got out of intensive care; perhaps she wasn't giving the green light – although, these days, Twigs claims she was disappointed that I didn't ask for her number, but she's got to say that! Anyway, five days later I went to the newsagent's for my morning paper and this big blue Jag – with an exquisite blonde inside – pulled up by the kerb. It was Twiggy. She wound down the window and said: 'Do you want a cup of tea?' Even I knew this was the green light!'

Every story of how two people met and fell in love is interesting, so give yourself permission to enjoy your own. With luck, there will be things to tease each other about (notice how Leigh does it over asking for the telephone number and Twiggy over the magazine interview) which in turn can develop into general, affectionate everyday banter between the two of you.

Start Asking in a Clear and Effective Way

Once the atmosphere between you and your partner has improved, try a small step towards better cooperation by asking for something directly. Although this might be a risky step, your chances of success are greater than you imagine.

Francis Flynn is the Associate Professor of Organisational Behaviour at Stanford University in California; he did three studies where people were asked to estimate the likelihood that others would agree to a direct request for help. These included people asking strangers if they could borrow a mobile phone, if they could escort them to a specific nearby destination and if they would make donations to a charity. He discovered that we underestimate our chances of success by a staggering 50 per cent.

The following tips will help boost the likelihood of getting a pleasant surprise to your request for help:

1. **Make it something small.** Remember, the aim is to tiptoe past your partner's fears.
2. **Keep the stakes low.** For the first request, make it a one-off: Could you pass me the

newspaper? Could you cut some mint from the garden for me? Avoid something that you want desperately and would be upset about if your partner refused.

3. **Double-check.** Is it a fair request? Is it easy for my partner to achieve?

4. **Choose your time.** If your partner is about to rush out of the door or is deep into some task, he or she will be less likely to stop and help. So don't sabotage the request before you've even begun by asking at the wrong moment.

5. **Don't dress it up.** Forget the preambles like 'I don't often ask, but . . .' or 'I know you're busy, but . . .' or explanations about why you need help: 'I'm really behind with this recipe and you know they're always early . . .' The danger is that your partner will have switched off before the request is made, have heard the preamble as an attack, or been unwittingly handed an excuse for not cooperating. So keep it simple: 'Please could you . . .?'

6. **Be prepared to try again.** Persuasive people don't let one mishap stop them. It often takes one or two attempts to ask in a clear and effective way.

Summing Up

When we are unhappy, we think the answer is to make big changes. Unfortunately, this sort of revolution is frightening for our partners who will either fight back or bury themselves in work, hobbies and looking after the children. Many people think the only alternative is to do nothing, but this leads to a feeling of hopelessness – fatal in the long term – or resentment. The answer, however, is to find a middle way: do less. Small steps allow a relationship to evolve and grow because they are unthreatening and therefore bypass our natural fear of change.

IN A NUTSHELL:
- If a journey of a thousand miles must begin with the first step, what small step could you make towards changing your relationship?
- Slow change is better than no change at all.
- Be interested in the small details of your partner's life and create a positive atmosphere where trust can flourish.

STEP 3

THINK SMARTER

If we're honest, we can all name areas of our relationship that we'd like to improve. Perhaps your partner uses Saturday as a chance to pursue a favourite hobby while you'd prefer to spend the time together. Maybe you've fallen out over your partner's reluctance to share the cooking or you've given up trying to keep track of your finances because he or she loses all the receipts. It doesn't matter if it is something petty – such as the best place to keep the bin bags – or something as important as which school your children should attend; these long-running disputes about family, household management and social life can really grind down your relationship.

Unfortunately, the most common ways of dealing with them – complaining, nagging, sulking, blackmail, playing martyr or agreeing to one thing but doing another – are not only unpleasant and ineffective in the long term, but also exacerbate the problem. In the worst cases, couples end up having arguments about arguments. However, there is a new strategy that not only takes the heat out of long-running disputes but can also actually solve them too. It is called nudging.

Surprisingly, the idea comes originally from politics. Governments have realised that lecturing and legislating – even if it is something that we know is in our best interests, such as drinking less or putting money aside for our old age – not only puts our backs up but also makes us dig in our heels and become more committed to our harmful habits. This is why the book *Nudge: Improving Decisions About Health, Wealth and Unhappiness* (Yale University Press, 2008) by Richard H. Thaler and Cass R. Sunstein – two professors from Chicago University – has attracted a lot of interest.

Thaler and Sunstein call the concept 'Libertarian Paternalism'. Libertarian, because people should be free to do what they wish. Paternalism, because it is legitimate for governments to influence people's behaviour to make their lives longer, healthier and better. They write: 'To count as a mere nudge, the intervention must be easy and cheap to avoid. Nudges are not mandates.'

Therefore a school canteen putting fruit at eye level – where pupils are more likely to see and buy it – is a nudge; banning junk food is not.

As a marital therapist, I am used to helping couples who are stuck in the same demand/withdraw cycle as politicians. So I wondered: what would happen if my clients nudged rather cajoled, tricked or bullied each other into submission?

Harness the Power of the Nudge

I have adapted the concepts that underlie Libertarian Paternalism into four interlocking strategies. Which ones would work for you?

Choice architecture

What's the big idea? The 'choice architect' is the person who organises the context in which others make decisions. It could be a doctor describing different possible treatments or a supermarket manager who decides where stock is displayed in the store. Although we like to think these people are being neutral, they are making hundreds of small decisions which have a major impact on our behaviour. For example, the supermarket could put the healthiest options in the prime positions or the items that generate the most profit. The doctor could marshal the statistics so that patients elect for his or her field of speciality.

Put it into action: Overall, relationships aim to be fifty/fifty but there are areas where each partner is in charge. Naomi and Barry have been married for fifteen years and over that time have established clear roles. Naomi, for example, was responsible for organising their social life but would often end up doing activities she was not particularly keen on. So how could she nudge rather than dictate to Barry? First, we looked at how she described the options for the weekend. Research shows that the first name on a ballot paper and the first special described by a waiter do the best. Next, we cut back the number of possibilities so that she didn't overwhelm Barry with choice and allow him to fall back on the same old choices – such as 'taking it as it comes'. Finally, Naomi accepted that she was the Choice Architect and edited out the options that appealed to her less. 'Over the bank holiday weekend, I suggested we visited my parents who had hired a cottage by the sea or went to a concert and firework spectacular in the park. Previously, I might have added just hanging out at the local wine bar. Much to my surprise, he happily went to the concert and enjoyed it.' Barry was still free to choose – rather than being forced into going – but Naomi had nudged him away from the wine bar.

Breakthrough tip: Don't overstretch yourself and try to become the Choice Architect in areas where you have no control – such as what time your partner leaves work.

Resetting the default

What's the big idea? Although economists think of us as rational, weighing up all the options and making informed choices, we are often lazy, inconsistent, fail to act in our own self-interest and stick with the status quo. Companies understand this inertia and profit from it. For example, a subscription TV channel will offer a free trial offer but set up a default where you are automatically subscribed unless you cancel. Their retention rate is much higher than if the default is that customers have to opt in.

Put it into action: In contentious issues around the house, look at the default position. Both Sheena and John were, in theory, responsible for laundry, but when the basket was overflowing, the default was that Sheena would curse and set to. 'I don't generally mind, but I just wish he'd help when I'm really stressed,' she explained. However, she had underestimated the power of inertia: John would mean to help but would fall back into his usual evening routine of fixing a drink and settling down to watch television.

Instead of Sheena playing the martyr or bitching about the laundry, we arranged a nudge for John by setting a new, more equitable, default system: whoever came home first would automatically put on a load of washing. If Sheena was working late, this would invariably be John and, instead of being 'a favour', it became part of the relationship's status quo.

Breakthrough tip: Don't expect your partner to settle into the new routine straight away, it takes time to build up a helpful habit. So be patient and, if needed, add in the other strategies.

Framing the options

What's the big idea? How you inform people has a big effect on their behaviour. In the Petrified Forest National Park in Arizona, they needed to stop visitors taking souvenir samples home. In an experiment, they changed the signs every two hours between a negative message stressing the harm done by stealing pieces of petrified wood and a positive one asking for help to protect the forest. The positive signs were significantly more effective than the negative ones.

Put it into action: Instead of telling your partner to do something, you can nudge by framing a possible window of opportunity. Philip had fallen out with his teenage daughter after some clumsy remark about her weight. His wife, Mina, tried to patch things up, but Philip really needed to talk to his daughter himself. Unfortunately, he kept putting off a possibly nasty confrontation.

After discussing the nudge concept, Mina enabled the discussion by telling him: 'I'm going to be out this afternoon, so the two of you will be alone.' As Philip later explained: 'This planted the seed in my mind and helped me to psyche myself up.'

Breakthrough tip: Don't fall into the trap of introducing something in a negative way: 'I know you're not going to want to . . .', as most probably they will agree with you.

Incentives and feedback

What's the big idea? Local authorities like Tayside in Scotland have been encouraging smokers to quit in return for grocery vouchers. In California, householders were informed if they were below or above average in their energy consumption. Heavy users began to cut back and the positive effect was magnified when the energy company added a happy smiley symbol to bills heading in the right direction.

Put it into action: People underestimate the power of incentives because this strategy has failed them in the past. In most cases, they were not aware of the other elements of a successful nudge. Perhaps they have not targeted areas where they are truly the choice architect and had such poor default systems that they had to give countless incentives or praise and ended up devaluing them. However, if you have followed the other nudge strategies, even small rewards will have a big impact.

When giving positive feedback, thank your partner at the time but reinforce the message by communicating your appreciation a few days later too. This will make your praise seem more considered and not just a reflex action.

Breakthrough tip: Don't bribe your partner as this will make you resentful in the long term, and don't give false praise as this ultimately puts your partner's back up.

IT'S A NUDGE RATHER THAN A SHOVE WHEN . . .

1. You can defend your actions in public – otherwise it is sneaky manipulation.

2. Your partner has the freedom to opt out – otherwise it is an order.

3. You are up for your partner nudging you back – otherwise you are just being a control freak!

Two Ways of Thinking

Psychologists and neuroscientists have begun to agree on how our brains function: we think in two completely different ways. The first is called 'Automatic' and happens so quickly and instinctively that we don't even associate it with thinking – like ducking when a ball is thrown in our direction or smiling at a kitten walking across a piano keyboard.

Neuroscientists believe the Automatic System is associated with the oldest parts of the brain, inherited from our reptile ancestors. The second form of thinking is called 'Reflective' and is rational and self-conscious. The best way to explain the difference is that we use our Automatic System when speaking our mother tongue but our Reflective System when learning and speaking a foreign language. The following table explains more:

Automatic System	Reflective System
Gut reaction	Head
Uncontrolled	Controlled
Effortless	Effortful
Instinctive	Deductive
Fast	Slow
Unconscious	Self-aware
Trained by repetition	Open to rational argument

In many ways, we are open to nudges because they work on our Automatic System, where we respond instinctively, rather than weighing up the options with our Reflective System.

The downside of Automatic Thinking

We lead busy and complicated lives and don't have the time or the energy to analyse everything. Therefore we use lots of short cuts to process information quickly. For example, we rely on rules of thumb to work out the cost of something in a foreign currency – and get a shock when finally we receive our credit card statements – or stereotypes to guide our response to people (the elderly are frail, or young people are open to new ideas) where a moment's thought tells us that such sweeping generalisations are meaningless. In other words, we might unquestioningly rely on our Automatic System but it frequently lets us down.

When it comes to dealing with our partner, we underplay the importance of Automatic Thinking and overestimate the power of Reflective Thinking – especially when we're trying to change long-held prejudices. For example, Maggie had a hard time recovering from her husband's affair with a work colleague. 'Although Simon doesn't see her on a day-to-day basis, they come together on major projects like pitching new work to clients,' she explained. 'He'd agreed to let me know whenever they would be in contact but time after time, he's let me down.' The most recent occasion had been only a few days previously. 'I'd had a bad day and phoned Simon to let off steam but he seemed very distant and I knew something was wrong,' said Maggie.

'But I told you the truth when I got home,' said Simon. He had been in the car with his former affair partner. 'When the boss suggested that I give her a lift, I couldn't really say no.'

'You could have sent me a text so that I'd have known and I certainly wouldn't have poured out my heart when that woman could have overheard.'

'This is why I don't always tell. My only reward for being honest is grief, drama and a cold shoulder in bed.'

Maggie thought this was unfair. She could list lots of times when Simon had told her about some instance of contact and she'd just thanked him. Unfortunately, Simon's Automatic System – trained by repetition – expected a bad reaction. His Reflective System might have been able to recall the positive occasions, but the bad ones – because of their severity – had registered more strongly and deeply in his brain.

How to use this knowledge: Learn the importance of repeating your positive new behaviour and don't be disappointed if it takes a while for your partner to respond and for the Reflective System to take over from the Automatic.

The downside of Reflective Thinking

Our rational brain values words over everything else. If we can just make our case effectively and logically, we *must* be persuasive. However, communication is made up of much more than just words. Professor Albert Mehrabian of the University of California did some groundbreaking work in the sixties about how we communicate feelings and attitude. For face-to-face communication, he found that we use three main ways:

1. WORDS. Those we actually use when speaking.
2. MUSIC. The tone of voice, pace, pitch and volume.
3. DANCE. Our body language.

If these three components had to add up to 100 per cent of communication, how much in percentage terms do you think WORDS make up? Have a guess. (The answer is below, upside down.)

Dance 55 per cent.
Words 7 per cent; Music 38 per cent;

Jane and Christopher, from the previous chapter, had had a nasty row after he stopped in the middle of their lovemaking because he felt she was just going through the motions. 'I don't want her to do it just for me,' said Christopher. 'How do you think that makes me feel? I want her to be an equal partner.'

'I keep telling you: I want to sort this problem out just as much as you,' Jane snapped back at him.

I stopped her: 'What sort of message do you think you're giving Christopher?'

'That I want to sort out our problems?' Jane looked puzzled.

Using Reflective Thinking, she had imagined that her words alone had counted. However, the MUSIC and DANCE had been completely different. Her tone had been far from conciliatory – she almost spat the words out. Her body language had also been aggressive – she had leaned forward and her eyes were flashing with anger. This had been what Christopher had responded to.

How to use this knowledge: Make certain that your words, tone and body language match. If there is a difference between what you're saying and how you're acting, the other person is more likely to believe the MUSIC and DANCE than the WORDS. In most cases, it is better to tell your partner just how upset you feel – rather than let this knowledge leak out through your tone and body language. Once you've calmed down a little, then you can try and build a bridge with words – but not before.

PRIMING

This exercise combines both ways of thinking. It will not only influence your partner's Automatic System but will also encourage him or her to engage their Reflective System too.

1. Researchers have discovered that just asking people if they intend to do something actually increases the likelihood that they will. For example, being asked if you will vote increases the chance of your voting by 25 per cent, and being asked if you plan to buy a new car increases the likelihood by 35 per cent. In effect, just measuring behaviour gives a nudge in that direction.

2. So prime your partner's Automatic System by asking: 'When can you . . .?' 'Have you any idea

when you will be able to . . .?' (For example, chop back the hedge or speak to your mother about babysitting.)

3. Make certain that your body language is relaxed or neutral. If you're exasperated, your message will come across as: 'Isn't it about time that you . . .' Under these circumstances, it is better to choose another occasion or your attempt to prime will be interpreted as nagging.

4. Encourage your partner to engage his or her Reflective System by asking: 'Is there anything that I can do to help?' This will allow him or her to consider possible obstacles and think through the best way to tackle the task: 'It would help if you could collect the children from swimming so I could get an early start on the hedge' or 'I'm really busy, would you mind phoning my mother?'

In action: Pascal and Hannah would argue about renovating their Victorian townhouse. 'He will have agreed to finish sanding the floor but it's always "Just let me finish this beer" or "I'm watching this crucial lap in the Grand Prix",' explains Hannah. 'We end up having terrible rows because I keep tripping over the equipment. Surely he can just get on and do it and then watch television?'

Her partner, Pascal, would have every intention of sanding the floor but get side-tracked by momentary pleasures, and soon it would be too late to start. The situation had deteriorated to such a point that Hannah thought, 'He doesn't care about my feelings' and Pascal thought Hannah was 'unreasonable'.

Instead of getting angry, I helped Hannah to prime Pascal by asking: 'Are you going to work on the floor this weekend?' and following up with: 'Are you going to ask your brother for help?'

However, don't get carried away with priming, to the point that your partner pictures an order with deadlines and penalty clauses, and be flexible enough so that your partner can set his or her own timetable.

Negotiating

With a better understanding of how we think and how we make decisions, it is time to look at what happens when our partner wants one thing and we want another. Is it possible to nudge him or her towards our way of thinking?

We spend a lot of time negotiating with our partner. Which restaurant will we eat at? Which movie shall we see? What time should our daughter be back home? Unfortunately, just doing something frequently doesn't necessarily make us any good at it. Especially as, when the discussion goes seamlessly, we are not really aware of what helped us reach agreement and, when it goes wrong, we are angry, frustrated or resentful towards our partner and not in the mood to explore our mistakes. So for many people negotiating is a bit of a mystery.

There are, in effect, two types of negotiating. The first is called 'Opposing' and it's competitive. Each side tries to get as close to their preferred outcome as possible. A classic example would be going into a car sales room: you want the lowest price and the best benefits while the owner wants to make the largest profit. The second is called 'Cooperative' and the main focus is reaching a mutually beneficial agreement. For example, the management needs to make savings – or the company will no longer be financially viable – but the union wants to protect jobs.

So how do these two types of negotiating work when dealing with your partner?

Opposing

This style of negotiating can easily go wrong:

Each partner takes up an extreme position

↓

One partner offers a tiny concession

↓

The other does the same

↓

Each partner keeps justifying
his or her position

↓

It becomes harder to change

↓

A battle of wills ensues

↓

Each partner defends his or her position
or makes an even smaller concession
to keep the negotiations alive

↓

Each partner becomes more stubborn
and focused on his or her position, not
on what is good for the relationship

↓

Result = No agreement or a poor one

In action: Mark and Sarah had been married for seven years and had two small children. Mark's passion in life was playing golf. In fact, he had wanted to be a professional but things hadn't worked out and he had taken an office job. 'I don't begrudge Mark his golf,' said Sarah, 'I know he needs to unwind but it really eats into family time.'

Both partners had taken an extreme position before coming into counselling. Mark wanted to be able to play on some Sundays: 'There're a couple of competitions that are being run at the club and I'd like to take part.' Sarah was horrified: 'I'm not that keen on you playing every Saturday, but Sundays too? We wouldn't see you at all. Couldn't we have just one or two golf-free week-ends for a change?'

Mark offered a small concession: 'I could start earlier and that way I'd be back for lunch and we'd still have the afternoon.'

However, both Mark and Sarah kept justifying their positions: 'I work really hard and this is my one bit of fun,' he said. 'The children are small and they *want* to do things with us at the moment,' she countered.

Next they started defending their positions: 'I let you go away on that golfing weekend,' said Sarah.

'It was my brother's stag do, I could hardly tell them "My wife won't let me come",' Mark replied.

Sarah was back on the attack: 'So you waited for the last possible moment to tell me – although you'd known for months.'

Mark replied: 'Do you wonder, with the amount of grief that I get?'

The subject became so toxic that we stopped discussing golf in their counselling sessions and focused on less controversial issues.

Cooperative

While you are in opposing negotiations your partner is part of the problem; with cooperative negotiations he or she is part of the solution:

Neither party puts a request on the table but instead discusses the issue at hand

↓

Each party explains their interests and needs

↓

Both listen with respect, whether they agree or not

↓

They look for common and shared interests

↓

Many possible approaches are discussed

↓

Each party focuses on finding a solution
rather than on promoting their favoured position

↓

Result = Agreement

In action: Further into counselling, Mark and Sarah tried to discuss golf again but instead of restating their positions, they talked about weekends together that had been a success. 'I enjoy going places with you and the kids,' said Mark, 'we've had some lovely days out.' Sarah agreed that things had been much better: 'I haven't minded so much about the golf – especially since you've been going earlier – and I've been able to get on with the chores.'

Next they explained their interests. 'Golf is important to me but so is my family,' said Mark. 'That's why I work so hard to pay for nice things.' 'I want you to be happy and I do appreciate everything that you do for us,' Sarah replied, 'but I want you to get the best out of our children.'

From this position, it was not difficult to find some common goals: being good parents, enjoying family trips, each needing their own time.

They discussed Sarah having a night to play sport during the week and how Mark could use that night to catch up with his paperwork – rather than Sunday nights.

Ultimately, they made no hard-and-fast deal. Mark did play in competitions – which occasionally meant going to golf on both Saturday and Sunday. However, he made up for it by skipping golf one weekend and taking the whole family camping instead. He also started taking odd days off during the school holidays for family trips rather than just reserving them for golf. By using cooperative negotiation, they could deal with each golfing case on its own merits.

NEGOTIATING TIPS

It is often easier to introduce Cooperative Negotiating when the stakes are low, so either practise at work or find an uncontroversial topic with your partner.

- Indicate clearly your needs and interests.
- Remember the old saying: 'If you don't ask, you don't get.'
- Listen carefully to the other person; repeat back their position so that you can be clear that you've fully understood.

- Just because the other person asks for something, it doesn't mean you necessarily have to give it.
- Look for common ground.
- People prefer to buy than be sold to. By this I mean we like to choose rather than have a particular option rammed down our throat.
- Stress your desire to reach agreement. For example, 'I'm confident that we can find something that will work for both of us' or 'We're not that far apart.'
- Remind each other of what you agree about – if only in principle at this stage.
- Leave something in reserve – especially in business dealings – so that you have a way of closing the deal.
- When you've reached agreement, repeat what you're going to do. This is partly because it ensures there are no misunderstandings but it also reminds both parties what has been achieved.

Summing Up

Nudging takes into consideration how people behave in the real world rather than how we'd like to believe they do. We are influenced by lots of seemingly insignificant decisions and decide on a course of action as much emotionally as rationally. This is why words alone are never enough to convince our partners about contentious issues – especially if our words are at odds with the tone of our voice or our body language.

IN A NUTSHELL:

- If you slip into a competitive style of negotiating, you are probably too focused on your own needs. If you are too quick to accommodate, you are too focused on your partner's needs. However, when you are compromising, you are aware of both of your needs.

- If negotiations become fraught, tell your partner how you're feeling – even if it is angry or frustrated – rather than suppressing your emotions. This helps your partner understand the effect his or her actions are having on you.

- Don't shut down any solution – however off-the-wall or impractical – because discussing it can easily lead to a great suggestion.

STEP 4

CARROTS RATHER THAN STICKS

So far, you have stopped using unsuccessful strategies for gaining cooperation and improved the overall atmosphere at home. You have made small but significant changes in your relationship and thought smarter about how to influence your partner. But what if you have been unhappy for a long time and feel only a revolution will solve your problems? What if your partner is either happy enough with the status quo or in denial about the extent of your misery? Don't worry, it is possible for one partner to initiate change. The next step will show you how.

One of the oldest debates is which works best: the carrot or the stick? Marcial Losada, an organisational psychologist from Michigan, US, decided to test this proposition. He observed businesses and, on the basis of results, customer satisfaction and opinions of managers and peers, he divided the staff into high, mid and low performers. Losada found that the high performance divisions used up to five times as many positive comments (carrots) than negative one (sticks). In sharp contrast, the poor performing teams gave significantly more negative statements than positive.

John Gottman, emeritus professor at the University of Washington, has studied how couples interact for over thirty years and claims to be able to predict with 94 per cent accuracy which newly-weds will remain married and which will divorce four to six years later. He stresses the importance of positive strokes too, i.e., compliments, 'thank-you's, reassurances, recognition of the other's viewpoints. We imagine that one unpleasant gesture – such as criticism or a complaint – can be cancelled out by one positive stroke. However, Gottman's findings suggest that our instincts are wrong. Couples who stay married will balance one negative with five positives, while couples who divorce can often have ten negatives to one positive.

With all the research pointing to five carrots to one stick as the optimum balance, how do you achieve this goal? Increasing the ratio of positives does not mean becoming unbearably cheerful or making up compliments – as this can come across as false. Instead, focus on communicating more effectively. Most people feel hundreds of positive emotions about their friends and work colleagues every day: 'It's nice to see you' or 'I really admire the way that you handled that.' Unfortunately, we keep most of these thoughts to ourselves. So try an experiment and tell your partner about these private positives. After seven days, stop and assess the atmosphere at home:

- How has it improved?
- Is your partner more willing to cooperate?
- How do you feel?

SO HOW DO YOU COME ACROSS AS POSITIVE?

- **Smile.** This will make you seem not only warm but also approachable.
- **Maintain good eye contact.** People who cannot look us directly in the eye are considered to be lying or trying to hide something.
- **Think positive thoughts.** We like people who make us feel good about the world and, most important of all, about ourselves. Someone who criticises, even if it is about something inconsequential like the decor, might be perceived as clever, intelligent or funny but we

> are always wary. Deep down, we fear they will be equally cutting about us behind our backs or, worse still, that the criticism is an indirect attack on our tastes or our personality.
>
> - **Appear interested.** Repeat back key phrases so that the person speaking knows you have been listening ('So he stepped right out in front of you?') and, most powerful of all, identifying feeling ('You must have been horrified').

Start With Small Carrots

Although this step in my programme focuses on making bigger changes, it is still important to lay the groundwork first. Here are two small but positive strategies for getting your partner to open up and allow you to understand him or her better:

Encouraging body language

- Leaning slightly towards someone – although not too close so that their personal space is invaded – shows interest.
- Crossing your arms will make you look defensive, so keep an open posture.
- Nodding signals not just encouragement but

demonstrates involvement in the story that you're being told. However, be aware that we normally nod in pairs. Three nods suggests that you wish to interrupt.

- Blinking can set a romantic mood. We blink every two or three seconds and increasing the rate will increase your partner's too. Conversely, slowing down a blink to a third of its natural speed can be sexually attractive as it mimics a wink.

- Mirroring – where you match your body posture to someone else's – can amplify any intimacy that is growing between two people.

- Babies love the game 'peek-a-boo' – where you hide your face behind your hand and then suddenly appear from nowhere. They will play it over and over without ever seeming to get bored. Adults who are interested in each other play a very similar game: looking at someone, then looking away and back again. They also use props like menus to disappear behind and then suddenly appear.

Encouraging easy, flowing conversation

- Value small talk. It is a good way of warming up for a more interesting conversation and provides a breathing space to relax and unwind after a tough day. So make a mental note of opening subjects that are non-controversial. For example: weather, recent news story, celebrity goings-on and television programmes.

- The secret of good conversation is to offer small snippets of self-disclosure. Don't just say that you've had a busy day – talk about a particular project or what your son or daughter has been doing.

- Look for areas of conversational connection. What might interest your partner? What could prompt him or her to ask questions?

- Echo your partner's language. If he is a teacher and calls his pupils 'kids', using the same word as he does will help increase your connection. If she is a businesswoman and refers to her 'firm', don't subsequently call it a 'company' as this will put up a conversational barrier.

- Don't block topics. You might not be particularly interested in the new out-of-town shopping centre or the allotment, but listening attentively shows that you value your partner and consider his or her activities interesting.

- Never underestimate the importance of asking questions. Everybody likes talking about themselves and their interests. A good listener will always be appreciated. So as well as offering your snippets of self-disclosure, be ready to take up your partner's too.

- Once you and your partner are talking freely about day-to-day news and can bring up day-to-day issues, it is much easier to move on to significant problems or unburden your heart.

Bigger Carrots

It is human nature to repay favours. Across all cultures, and throughout history, doing something for someone else effectively puts them in our debt and encourages them to return the favour as soon as possible.

A good example is a classic experiment carried out by Dr Dennis Regan from Cornell University who gathered volunteers, supposedly to measure art appreciation, in teams of two. Unknown to the volunteers, their partner for the test was his assistant. Halfway through, the assistant would explain that he was thirsty and ask to go off and buy a can of soda. On some occasions, he would return with a second can for his partner too. After the test had finished, the assistant announced that he was selling raffle tickets for charity. The teammates who had been given the can of soda were twice as likely to buy tickets – even though they cost much more than the price of the drink.

This idea of reciprocity was also studied by Francis Flynn, whom we met earlier, from Stanford University. The staff at an airline customer service desk were permitted to swap shifts and this allowed Flynn to look at favours in the real world rather than an artificial situation in the laboratory. His work found a significant difference between the recipient of the favour and the person doing the favour. The recipient valued the favour the most immediately afterwards. Over time, the benefits – for example, being able to attend their child's school play – receded into a distant memory and became less valuable. Conversely, the favour-doer placed a low value on agreeing to cover the shift at the time – 'no problem' – but gave a greater value to the favour as time passed.

This research demonstrates the gulf that opens when there is no opportunity to return the favour within a reasonable time-frame. While the recipient has possibly forgotten the incident, the favour-doer is left holding a growing grudge.

So how can you use this research?

- **Understand the importance of favours.** Although, in theory, we do things for love, marriage and long-term relationships are effectively a complex web of favours given and returned.

- **Understand the nature of favours.** A favour is a one-off kindness. When something becomes a regular occurrence, it will slide from a favour into an entitlement. So although cooking your partner's favourite meal is a nice thing to do – and would definitely count as a carrot – it is unlikely to be a favour (unless cooking is normally your partner's responsibility).

- **Reciprocate as soon as possible.** If your partner does not ask for a favour, offer to go that extra mile for him or her. For example: 'Would you like me to collect you from your girls' night so that you don't have to bother about finding a taxi?' or 'I'll take your mother to the hospital so that you can go to golf.'

- **Keep the favours at a sensible size.** With the reciprocal nature of favours, we feel over-whelmed if our partner does something too big and fear it is impossible to repay.

- **Understand that favours in the rear-view mirror can seem bigger.** This is another reason to keep favours to manageable proportions as your partner will be most grateful at the time, but you will value the favour more over time and could become resentful. The following story illustrates this point:

When Peter and Jackie came into counselling, the air was thick with distrust and resentment. So I investigated what Peter had done for Jackie and vice versa.

'My aunt died two years ago and left me a significant amount of money,' said Peter, 'but as things were not that good between us, I thought I'd throw a big surprise fortieth birthday party for Jackie.' He also bought her an extravagant present. In his mind, these favours meant that he would stop getting 'grief' from his wife.

Jackie saw things differently: 'I'm not saying that I didn't enjoy the party. It was wonderful, but if you'd discussed it with me, I'd much rather we'd spent the money on something practical – like new windows for the house.' In effect, Peter's favour to Jackie – in the rear-view mirror – still appeared big to him but to her it appeared so small, it was invisible (unless she was reminded).

Suddenly, in the counselling room, Jackie became angry:

'If you were trying to buy me with that jewellery, you can take it back to the shop right away.'

'It was a present. Don't be stupid,' he replied.

This dispute underlines the importance of small and medium-sized, rather than big, carrots. Nobody wants to feel bought or too in debt.

CARROTS AND STICKS IN ACTION

Getting your partner to say 'yes' is all about finding the appropriate carrots, but that doesn't mean there isn't a place for an occasional small stick:

1. **Instead of criticising what you don't like, praise what you do like.** When training my puppy, Flash, I would much rather he did his 'business' on the open fields behind our house rather than on the streets where I would have to pick up after him. So if he went on the grass verge, I would make him sit while I got out a bag. If he waited an extra five minutes and went under a hedgerow, I would offer lots of praise. Within a few weeks, he always went in the countryside.

2. **Keep reinforcing good behaviour.** When my puppy stole a shoe and ran around the house with it, I'd ignore him, so he quickly tired of that game. If he took a snooze in the sun at the top of the stairs, I would praise and stroke him. In this way, I rewarded the quiet behaviour that allowed me to get on with my writing and did not reward bad behaviour with negative attention. It might take a while for your partner to put his or her coffee cup in the dishwasher, but make a point of saying 'Thank you, I really

appreciated that' rather than ignoring him or her or saying something sarcastic.

3. **Make your intervention timely.** Dogs live in the moment, so if you find a chewed shoe – even if you put it under their nose – they cannot associate the telling-off with their action. In the dog's mind, he has been lying down quietly, minding his own business, and for some unknown reason he's in trouble. However, if you catch him with the shoe in his mouth, this is the perfect time to say 'no'. Humans have a better sense of time than dogs, but getting upset about something that happened weeks ago is pointless and, in the same way, praising the behaviour that you like is more powerful in the moment too.

4. **Small reprimands can work.** When Flash was still a young puppy, I took him to my writers' group. After lunch, I walked him round and round the nearby park, giving him his instruction to empty his bladder – without success. I took him round my friend's garden, still no luck. Finally, I gave up and returned inside. Two minutes later, he squatted down in her living room and relieved himself. Without thinking, I took him by the scruff of the neck, shook him like a bitch

would discipline her puppies, and then placed him outside. He never repeated this behaviour in my house or anybody else's. The intervention worked because the punishment was small, timely and over quickly. Small sticks that will work with your partner might include a disapproving look or a complaint ('Please don't . . .').

Appreciative Inquiry

The regular way to solve a problem is to look at what has gone wrong and to seek a solution. However, in the eighties, businesses, which wanted to change and renew, started to embrace an idea called Appreciative Inquiry. Rather than fixing problem areas, AI (Appreciative Inquiry) focuses on building on what already works. AI practitioners believe this approach makes staff more creative, increases trust and brings out the basic goodness in people. By contrast, problem-solving just encourages blame and fault-finding.

Recently, I have started using these techniques with clients who are stuck in a rut because it fits with my philosophy that carrots work better than sticks. But before I explain how you can use AI, let's look at how it works in the business setting.

Every intervention has to fulfil four criteria:

Appreciative: What assets does a company have? What does it do well?

Applicable: Staff tell stories of past successes and the emphasis is on practical ideas and finding the best of what is currently happening.

Proactive: People are invited to imagine what the future might be like and how to redesign the organisation to bring about these aspirations. With a positive atmosphere, staff can take risks and share every possible solution.

Collaborative: Everybody is involved from the senior management right down to the youngest and most junior member of staff.

The last aspect is probably one of the reasons why AI works so well. Although nobody likes change being imposed, if we are involved from the start, have our say, are listened to and become part of the team that finds the solution, we will not only go along with any innovations but also positively embrace them. The following diagram shows how AI works in practice:

Discover what works
(In as much detail as possible)

Deliver
(How can we sustain
these changes?)

Dream
(What might be)

Design
(Co-constructing)

AI and your relationship

This process works best when there is a long-running or difficult issue to resolve. Start by agreeing to put all negatives to one side for the next hour. (If anything negative does come up, write it down and discuss it on another occasion.) Next work your way round the AI circle:

Discover what works
- Tell each other stories about the good times in your relationship.
- Think of the peak experiences or the high points. In those experiences, discuss the things that you valued most about a) yourself and b) your partner.

- Ask each other: What was good about those times? Probe deeper. What else was good about them?
- Think about the core factors that give 'life' to your relationship and the other positive values on which to build.

Dream
- What three wishes would heighten the health and vitality of your relationship?
- Put your energy into listening to your partner's ideas rather than debating them.
- Give each other time and space to dream in detail.
- If anything was possible, how would you like your relationship to be?
- What is important to you? Why do you care about it?

Design
- What would help you reach this goal?
- What skills can you each draw on?
- How can you help each other?
- What do you both agree on?

Deliver
- What is the next step?
- How could you reach that goal?

- What problems might occur?
- How could you overcome them?
- How would you know that things have been resolved?
- What do you need to talk about at a future occasion?

AI in action

Gemma and Paul had been together for three years but Paul had a child from a previous relationship. Unfortunately, his ex still had strong feelings for him and would frequently text – either messages of 'undying love' or 'goodbye for ever'. It was creating a lot of tension between Gemma and Paul. 'I have to keep on friendly terms with my ex or she could make it very difficult for me to see my son,' explained Paul. 'Except I never know when he's going to get a text and whether his bad mood is because of a work problem, something I've done or another text from her,' said Gemma. 'It's like she can come into my house any time she wants.' The ex-partner's destructive behaviour had moved up a gear since Paul and Gemma had married. Although there were plenty of problems to explore, I decided to put those to one side and to focus on Appreciative Inquiry.

So in **Discover what works**, I asked about a time when Paul and Gemma had had a good discussion about his ex. 'He'd been very down – a bit of food poisoning – and I asked him whether he was feeling better and he opened up about the latest text,' said Gemma.

'She wanted me to go to the beach with her and our son because "fathers should teach their children to swim". It had really upset me.' Instead of having their usual disagreement or fight, this time they'd ended up having a cuddle instead.

Next, in **Dream**, Gemma and Paul discussed how they would like things to be. 'I don't want her to keep coming between us,' said Paul, 'so we can focus more on what's really important: you and me.'

Gemma had a wish: 'I'd like you to tell me more about the texts.'

At this point, I had to intervene or they would have gone into their regular negative territory (where Paul complained that Gemma got wound up and angry over the texts and she would complain it was because she was continually excluded). Fortunately, they accepted that under AI their usual rows were banned. Gemma, instead, gave us another positive dream: 'I'd like to get to know your son better and for the three of us to spend more time together.'

With **Design**, we looked at what had worked when they'd talked and then cuddled. 'I was open and timely about the text,' said Paul. 'Normally I would have stewed over it or told Gemma weeks later.'

'I acknowledged how upsetting it is not to see much of his son or to be there to teach him to swim,' said Gemma. 'I also stopped to process the information before reacting.' Instead of assuming that Paul wanted to go to the beach with his ex and his son – as she might have done when things were bad between her and Paul – Gemma had checked it out.

'It would be entirely inappropriate for me to go the beach with her and, anyway, the only person I want to be with is you,' said Paul.

Finally, in **Deliver**, they discussed how to make their dream of better communication regarding Paul's ex come true. After explaining why he normally kept the texts to himself – 'I don't want to break her confidences' – Paul decided to forward them on to Gemma for a trial period. Although she had asked for this outcome before, it emerged naturally out of the AI process because Paul had been involved in reaching this conclusion, rather than having it imposed. Meanwhile, Gemma agreed to bring up only the most pressing texts and pledged her continuing support for Paul.

Another example of AI in action is Nicholas and Miranda, both in their forties, who came into counselling because they had drifted apart. Instead of looking at the problems in their relationship, I focused on what was working. They both had successful careers and two children who were eleven and nine. 'I enjoy the time we spend together,' said Miranda, 'but we don't get to do it that often because we're both tired.' I stopped her – as she was about to cross over into the negative – and encouraged her to tell me the story of a good time.

'I helped the children make pancakes in the kitchen and Nicholas laid the table and ran to the corner store for honey. Our youngest had trouble tossing her pancake and Nicholas helped and teased her that it would hit the ceiling,' said Miranda.

'The children were finally exhausted and went up to bed early. Instead of clearing up, we opened a bottle of wine and put some music on and slow danced,' added Nicholas.

So I encouraged them to start to **Dream** about how life might be in ten years' time. 'I really want to have a future with you,' said Nicholas.

Miranda visibly relaxed. I asked her why?

'I sometimes thought he was there out of habit, convenience.'

'It's good to hear it said out loud?' I asked.

She nodded.

In **Design**, Nicholas decided to work on his weight: 'I really want to be around to enjoy a long future with Miranda and a healthy one too.'

Suddenly Miranda was able to get away from work more often and in **Deliver** they managed more weekends away in the countryside.

APPRECIATIVE INQUIRY QUIZ

AI is built around thought-provoking questions that focus attention on what works and opens up discussion on how to build on success. This is why the wording has to be carefully thought through. Look at the following questions or prompts and decide which are the best-framed.

1. In general, which is the best way to start a discussion about a topic?
   a) Yes/No option
   b) How?
   c) What if?
   d) Which?
   e) Who?
   f) What?
   g) When?
   h) Why?
   i) Where?

2. When talking about the future of your children, which best suits Appreciative Inquiry?
   a) Are our children getting the best education?
   b) Describe a time when our children were flourishing at school.
   c) What supports their learning?
   d) Why do they sometimes get poor grades?
   e) What would it be like if . . .?

Answers

Question one: 'What if?' is probably the best way of framing a question because it invites our partner to dream.

'How?' and 'What?' are excellent for focusing your discussion.

'Which?', 'Who?', 'What?', 'When' are all good too.

Be careful about 'Why?', as it can either make your partner defensive (it can be interpreted as blame) or if he or she doesn't have a definitive answer, the discussion is shut down before it starts. So try substituting, 'Why?' with 'What are the contributing factors?'.

The least successful frame will prompt a Yes/No answer and narrow rather than broaden the discussion.

Question two: Although all the questions could have prompted a discussion, some are better than others. I have listed them from most to least helpful:

e) This is a great prompt because it fulfils the first part of the AI: **Discover what works.**

b) Another winner because it opens up the discussion.

c) This is an OK question because it is open. However, it can also be a sneaky way of introducing a favoured outcome. (For example: 'What would it be like if we got them some private tuition?') This could close down the conversation too quickly and not allow time for other, possibly better, options to emerge.

d) Unfortunately, 'Why' questions encourage fault-finding and blame. (For example, 'The grades are poor because you don't help them enough with their homework' or 'They mix with the wrong crowd'.)

a) This is the least successful question as it prompts a Yes/No or Agree/Disagree answer.

Summing Up

When we focus on what doesn't work, we not only take for granted what does work, but also treat it as normal and therefore don't truly understand the pleasures and resources of our relationship. Remembering the good times can help you dream and rediscover your desire for each other. In general, carrots (positives) provide a better incentive for change than sticks (negatives). However, be wary of offering too big a favour as nobody likes to be bribed.

IN A NUTSHELL:

- Don't keep positive feedback to yourself.
- When something goes smoothly, go back over it in your mind's eye. What helped make it a success? How could you build on that for the future?
- We resist change when it is done to us rather than with us. So involve your partner in your dreams.

STEP 5

CHANGE YOUR BEHAVIOUR

At the beginning of the book, I claim the art of persuasion is as much about changing how you come across as changing your partner. In my workshops, a lot of people are sceptical; they are much keener to concentrate on getting their partner to do what they want. However, the way our behaviour affects our partner's behaviour is one of the most important ideas in my programme and that's why I've devoted a whole chapter to the subject.

In the previous steps, you've discovered that if you come across in an aggressive manner, your partner responds in a similarly aggressive manner – and fights back either overtly (and triggers a nasty row) or covertly (by agreeing to your face but subverting behind your back). If you come across as passive and pleading, your partner will either ignore your request or become exasperated.

However, if you ask in an open and direct manner, he or she will respond in a similarly open way. In other words, our behaviour and that of our partner is inextricably linked.

So next time you're frustrated by your partner's stubbornness, unwillingness to open up or some particularly annoying habit, don't focus on his or her half of the equation, but look at your half instead. After all, as the old saying goes: 'The only person you can change is yourself'.

Achieving Balance

Most people arrive at my counselling office with complaints about their partner's behaviour. A typical example is Julie, thirty-three, whose husband had cheated on her with a woman fifteen years older on seven or eight occasions during their six-year marriage: 'I'm finding it difficult to understand his motive. When I ask the usual searching questions – "Is she better in bed, more attractive?" – you would think I had asked him to drink a cup of cold sick. I am seriously querying my own judgement. I can't believe I've given birth to this man's child and he has the cheek to cheat on me! I have been tempted to get my revenge but haven't risen to it, but I have to say that all bets are off.' After getting that off her chest, Julie took a deep breath and asked: 'Why won't he open up to me?'

I asked her to describe her husband.

'He is the type of person who is terrible at showing his emotions,' she said.

'What about you?'

'I'm fairly confrontational and particularly good at putting people on the spot. In fact, I've given him an ultimatum that before I decide whether I can continue with our relationship I need an explanation as to why he has never been faithful.'

Faced with this threat, it was not surprising that her husband had trouble opening up. I asked Julie if there was any connection between her being 'confrontational' and her husband being 'terrible at showing emotions'. She did a double take. Quite understandably, Julie had been concentrating on her husband's unacceptable behaviour and did not realise how her communication style was making him clam up.

Another person unaware of the link between her behaviour and her partner's was Paula. Her husband, Jeff, had announced that he was unhappy and, to her immense frustration, could not decide whether he wanted to try and save the marriage or leave. Not surprisingly, she was confused: 'One moment I'm up, one moment I'm down. If we're watching television, I wonder if I should be saying something but then I'm worrying about forever bringing up our problems and making him angry. In the meantime, there is an awkward silence. Should I say something? Should I stay quiet?' While Paula was turning herself inside out trying to fix the problems in her marriage, what was her husband doing? 'He just mopes about the house and occasionally moans: "I've been a terrible husband. I've been a terrible father." I try to reassure him but it does no good.' In fact, Jeff was sinking deeper into depression. Although he had triggered the problem, Jeff had no need to put any thought or energy into solving it because Paula had taken all the responsibility for fixing things between them.

I ask people like Julie and Paula to imagine that they are on a see-saw. The more they push down on their side – pushing for an answer or trying to fix their relationship – the more their partner flies up on the other side. In Julie's partner's case, this was closing down and in Paula's, Jeff became even less interested in finding a solution.

So what's the answer? Instead of retreating into an exaggerated, almost cartoon version of yourself, head towards the middle of the see-saw as this will allow your partner to give up his or her extreme position too.

Julie was sceptical: 'But if I don't push, I'll never get an answer.' However, she agreed to be less confrontational and to see what happened.

At the next week's session, she was all smiles: 'I just listened, nodded my head and kept quiet when he said something and somehow he opened up,' she explained. Her husband had had occasional problems maintaining an erection. 'He wanted to please me so much, this would make him anxious and he'd find it harder to perform. Because he didn't really care about the other woman, he didn't worry and had no problems – in some rather sick way, the sex with her made him feel more of a man.'

Although Julie did not particularly like her husband's answer, it did help her move on and begin to address the problems underlying her husband's affair. (For more help on this topic read my book *How Can I Ever Trust You Again?*)

Meanwhile, Paula took a step back and instead of trying to solve Jeff's unhappiness, she began to accept her own dissatisfaction with the marriage. 'We have both become very good at playing happy families,' she explained. Once she was honest about her issues, Jeff realised it was not all 'his fault' and decided to come into counselling. Instead of fixing the marriage being Paula's project, it became a joint one. They were no longer at opposite ends of a see-saw; they had achieved balance.

GETTING OFF THE SEE-SAW

Once you and your partner are polarised on opposite ends of a see-saw, it becomes harder and harder to change. This exercise will help break this unhelpful pattern:

1. **Recognise your see-saw.** Some of the common ones include: Bringing Up Problems/Containing Problems; Spender/Saver; Independence/Togetherness (one partner stresses the importance of 'me' time and the other 'us' time); Optimist/Pessimist. This is just a small selection. What is your see-saw?

2. **Accept the equal importance of your partner's position.** If a couple never brought up problems, nothing would get solved. However, if they argued about everything – and there was no sense of proportion – life would be equally impossible. Similarly, if a couple did nothing but spend, they would become bankrupt. However, if they were both keen on saving – and were unable to enjoy their money – life would be equally miserable. What are the advantages of your partner's position?

3. **Experiment.** Instead of retreating to your end of the see-saw and worrying, for example, that relaxing your grip on the purse strings will make your partner go crazy, discover what happens if you listen to your partner, hear his or her fears and find a joint solution.

4. **Become a little bit more like your partner.** This will allow him or her to change and become a little bit more like you.

Talking at Cross Purposes

If you're frustrated about your partner's actions but uncertain how your behaviour might be contributing, Transactional Analysis, or TA for short, can be a real eye-opener. In the 1950s, an American psychiatrist called Eric Berne proposed that all our thoughts, feelings and behaviour come from three distinct parts of our personality: 'Parent', 'Adult' and 'Child'. (The idea is similar to Freud's superego, ego and id.)

Christmas, for example, is one of the few times when all three parts of our personality come equally to the fore. We indulge our inner child with presents and allow its creativity free rein with decorations and party games. At the same time, our inner parent has a lot to organise and almost naturally slips into two types of behaviour. Berne calls these: Nurturing Parent (Don't worry, I'll buy a present for your mum) and Critical Parent (You've laid the table all wrong). Finally, we need the adult part of our personality, which is objective and rational, to help us navigate through all the alcohol, rich food and heightened emotions. Berne stresses the importance of all three parts of our personality and, indeed, keeping the 'Parent', 'Adult' and 'Child' in harmony makes for a well-rounded individual. The problem is how we use them to communicate with other people.

If you and your partner are both using the same parts of your personality, everything is fine. For example, at a boring party, your inner child meets the eye of your partner's inner child and both decide to put some music on and get everybody dancing. Berne calls this a *Concordant Transaction*.

P = Parent
A = Adult
C = Child

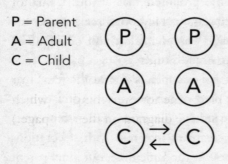

A variation on this relatively straightforward type of communication is when one partner's inner child complains: 'I'll never get all this done' and the other's nurturing parent replies: 'Never mind, I'll sort it out.' This is called a *Parallel Transaction* and, in theory, this kind of communication could continue happily for years.

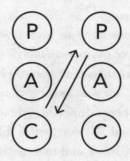

The problems come from what Berne calls *Crossed Transactions*. For example, the 'Adult' part of your personality asks: 'Have you seen my keys?' However, instead of replying with his or her inner adult, your partner responds: 'You shouldn't leave things lying about' – which is 'Critical Parent' – or 'Why do you blame me for everything?' – which is inner child. (See the diagram on the next page.)

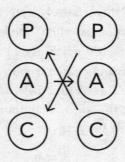

At this point, we need to look in more detail at the three parts of our personality. In the same way that there are two types of parent (Nurturing and Critical), there are also two types of child. Berne calls these the Free Child (the source of creativity, joy and fun) and the Adapted Child (which has learned to sulk, moan and manipulate). However, there is only one adult mode – which is rational and good at making decisions.

How to spot which part of your personality is in play

It is not just the words that betray which part of our personality is at the fore but the tone of our voice, facial expressions and general body language:

| | Parent | | Adult | Child | |
	Nurturing Parent	Critical Parent		Free Child	Adapted Child
Words	Let me help you, Don't worry, There-there	Should, Don't, You can't, If I were you	How, When, Why, What are the facts, options	Wow, Brilliant, You'll never guess	Sorry, If only, It's not my fault
Tones of Voice	Soothing, soft, caring, sympathetic	Stern, harsh, indignant, judgmental	Clear, enquiring, assertive	Laughing, energetic, excited	Appealing, placating, protesting
Body Language	Open arms, nodding, touching	Finger pointing, hands on hips, rolling eyes upwards	Level eye contact, confident appearance, active listening	Bright-eyed, exaggerated motions, spontaneous	Downcast eyes, pouting, slumped shoulders

TA in action

Once you can read which part of the personality is speaking and which is responding, how
can you use this knowledge to improve your
relationships? Mike and Alan are a gay couple
in their mid-thirties who have been together
for five years. Mike is very family orientated and
likes to go round to his parents for Sunday lunch
but Alan feels that Mike's parents do not really
accept their relationship.

'Why do I want to spend time with people
who barely tolerate me?' complained Alan.

'They're doing their best,' replied Mike.

'So why after all these years do you still need
to tell them to buy me a birthday present?' Alan
said, then turned to me. 'But what I really hate is
the way that he regresses to being ten years old
again when he's with his parents.'

Mike's parents were certainly in critical parent
mode; meanwhile, Mike himself was slipping into
one of the two types of inner child responses.

When I explained TA to this couple, they
immediately spotted that Mike was in adapted
child mode.

'See, it's what I've been telling you,' Alan said,
'and this has got to stop.'

'Which part of your personality is talking?' I asked.

Alan suddenly laughed as he recognised that this outburst came straight from his own critical parent.

Instead of having the same old argument, they both accessed their adult mode and decided it was better to invite Mike's parents round to their house. At the next counselling session, we used TA to examine what happened.

'My mother was a little snide about the mashed potatoes,' explained Mike. 'Rather than ignoring her or taking out my bad mood on Alan, I asked my mother: "Is there a problem?"' In effect, he had accessed the adult part of his personality. Interestingly, by not responding as a child, he encouraged his mother to move into adult mode too. They had a long chat later while clearing up, and she admitted that she felt uncomfortable that her son cooked, as she saw this as 'feminine'.

Another example of TA helping a couple is Daniel and Lorna. They are in their mid-forties and have a son who wanted to join the army. Daniel believed they should support their son's choice and Lorna wanted to do everything to protect him.

'You've always been overprotective and smothered him,' Daniel complained.

Lorna came straight back: 'Is it any wonder, with the way that you're always on at him: push, push, push. Nothing is ever good enough for you. Have you ever asked why he wants to get away from us?'

With Transactional Analysis, they recognised their two styles of parenting: nurturing (not always positive as it can prevent children taking responsibility for themselves) and critical (not always negative as it can push children to grow and achieve). Just as important, we looked at the type of parenting that Daniel and Lorna had received and how these experiences had fed into their behaviour today.

In fact, another way of looking at the three parts of our personality is that 'Parent' is life as we were taught, 'Child' is life as we feel it, and 'Adult' is life as we work it out for ourselves.

Although there are many different TA combinations, there are two crossed transactions that are particularly common in my counselling room:

My partner is behaving like a sulky teenager

'I already have two children, I don't need a third,' Sophie complained about her husband, Charlie. 'When he comes home in the evening, I'm exhausted but he seldom volunteers to help – not even with the fun stuff like bath-time. And if I ask him a question – like 'Is the water too hot?' – he either explodes or sulks.

Diagnosis: If your partner behaves like a child, it might be that you're treating him or her like one.

Solution: Come out of parent mode (probably critical parent) and talk adult-to-adult.

My partner is always talking down to me

'I asked my husband for help with my tax return and I got a lecture about keeping my paperwork straight,' said Kate. 'It went from bad to worse and he started complaining about my "attitude" but I'd just asked a simple question.'

Diagnosis: If your partner treats you like a child, it could be that you've been acting like one.

Solution: Shift into talking adult-to-adult.

How to communicate adult-to-adult

Being in adult mode means asking directly and openly for something (wheedling, manipulating and demanding are all childish behaviours). It means accepting our partner is equally capable and has similar or complementary skills (and therefore has a viewpoint that should be heard and respected). Adult behaviour is also rational, enquiring and open to negotiation.

For example, when Sophie examined her own behaviour – rather than focusing on Charlie's – she realised that she'd been super-vising him rather than asking for his help. When she relaxed and let him get on with bathing the children his way, her husband volunteered more often to take over. Meanwhile, Sophie could slowly switch over from being a mother into being one half of a couple. When bath-time was over, they would cuddle on the sofa or share a bottle of wine.

When Kate looked at her behaviour, she decided to get her paperwork straight and read the tax form before asking for help. In that way, she would have specific questions to ask her husband and have an adult-to-adult conversation.

There is more about good communication in another book in this series: *Resolve Your Differences.*

TA QUIZ

Being able to spot the different parts of our personality – critical parent, nurturing parent, adult, free child or adapted child – is the most important ingredient in changing our behaviour. So look at the following scenarios and decide which part of the personality is in play:

1. When Angela's friend was stood up by her boyfriend for the second time that month, Angela said: 'I told you he was trouble.'

2. When Carl's wife's best friend came round in a terrible state – her long-term boyfriend had left their shared house and moved in with another woman – he recommended a lawyer who could advise on her rights.

3. Brian didn't want to renovate the kitchen, he thought the current one was fine and, anyway, they couldn't afford a new one. However, his wife put so much pressure on him that he agreed to make a start. Except, he could never find the right weekend to start. There were always more pressing jobs and even the arrival of a new oven did nothing to speed him along.

4. When Patricia's brother-in-law died, she collected her sister from the hospice, took her home and fed her and then drove from place to place to make all the arrangements for the funeral.

5. When there was a power cut during an important dinner party and Susie couldn't melt the chocolate for her profiteroles, she put a pot over her open fire. Later she encouraged everybody to tell ghost stories.

Answers

These are the parts of the personality in play in the scenarios above:

5. *Free child*
4. *Nurturing parent*
3. *Adapted child*
2. *Adult*
1. *Critical parent*

It is worth pointing out that in the quiz, Angela, Carl, Patricia and Susie responded with the most appropriate mode of behaviour for their circumstances. There are times when we need someone to tell us we've made a mistake (critical parent) or to take over (nurturing parent). Free child is often fun and creative. Adult is rational and helps us take a considered look at a problem. Adapted child is more problematic. It can make us question authority and rebel against injustice but, in the example, Brian's procrastination just prolonged his problems rather than resolved them.

Ultimately, we need every one of these ways of responding in our toolkit. Problems arise when someone gets stuck in one mode.

People are OK

How we talk to our partner has a big impact on how our partner reacts. If we treat him or her well, he or she will return the favour. However, self-interest alone should not drive our behaviour – rather a fundamental belief that our partner deserves our respect. This is a second important idea embedded in Transactional Analysis: 'People Are OK'. By this, Berne means that everybody has worth, value and dignity. At first sight, this is not such a radical idea. However, while we're happy to sign up for 'worth, value and dignity' for all mankind, we're not necessarily so compassionate towards ourselves and our family. So while 'People are OK' at a universal level should translate down to the personal and relationship level as **'I'm OK, You're OK'** (which is the title of a famous book written by Thomas A. Harris, a long-term friend and associate of Berne), it often becomes:

I'm not OK, You're not OK
I'm not OK, You're OK
I'm OK, You're not OK

The impact of believing 'I'm not OK'

When, deep down, someone believes that they are '*not* OK', there are normally two ways of coping. The first is to accept the label – which has been pinned on by parents, teachers and lovers – and become depressed. The second is to fight back and expend a lot of energy trying to prove to yourself and to the world at large that you are 'OK' after all. Unfortunately, the internal picture of being 'not OK' is so strong that anything beyond top of the class, most talented newcomer, employee of the month or mum of the year equals complete failure. The only option is to strive harder and harder and become a perfectionist.

If it is tough being a perfectionist, it is even tougher being the partner of one. 'My husband hates mess so much that I make certain that the kids tidy up all of their toys half an hour before Vincent gets home,' says Mica. 'I'm reasonably tidy, I like to keep things straight, but he is fanatical.' Normally the partners of perfectionists are fairly laid-back – as it would be impossible for two perfectionists to live together – and do their best to accommodate their partner's whims. However, the obsessive behaviour can grind them down. 'Even Vincent's mates have a go at him – especially after he insisted on going home from the pub and getting changed after he got a bit of beer over his shirt,' says Mica.

If you're a perfectionist, ask yourself: Am I concentrating on my partner's behaviour to avoid looking at myself? When Vincent became more aware of his own behaviour and stopped trying to control Mica and his children, he couldn't help but focus on the high standards he set himself and how often he felt a failure. 'When I was a kid, my mother spent a lot of time making me look adorable. Little buttoned-up coat, polished shoes. She was always wiping my face with the corner of her handkerchief,' says Vincent. 'She would be so proud of me but she'd explode if I so much as stepped in a puddle or my school cap wasn't straight.'

'Did it seem that she only loved you when you were neat and tidy?' I asked.

Vincent didn't reply; he started crying.

Time and again, it seems that being a perfectionist is like carpeting the whole world to avoid getting a thorn in your foot – rather than putting on a pair of shoes. In other words, rather than trying to bend everybody else to your standards, put that energy into understanding yourself, giving yourself a little more leeway and developing a thicker skin so that when things don't or can't go your way, rejection does not feel so personal. There is more about improving self-esteem in another book in this series: *Learn to Love Yourself Enough*.

The impact of believing 'You're not OK'

If you believe your partner is not OK, you are going to want to change him or her. After all, you have plenty of evidence of bad or unsavoury behaviour and it is quite reasonable to want to make changes . . . or is it? Before you get angry and throw this book across the room, let me explain. If people have worth, value and dignity, then your partner must have those qualities too – but somehow you have become blinded to them.

So what's happening? Our common-sense understanding of the world sees a simple link between an event and how it makes us feel. For example, Gemma, from the previous chapter, would get upset every time Paul received a text from his ex.

Event ⟶ Emotion

Text ⟶ Upset

However, in reality, the picture is more complicated. There is no direct relationship between an event and emotion. Everything is filtered through our own particular interpretation. For example, Gemma thought that Paul was too friendly to his ex and that had encouraged her to hope for a reconciliation. She worried that his ex would 'forever' be interfering in their marriage and that this would 'spoil' everything.

Event ⟶ Interpretation ⟶ Emotion

Text ⟶ Ruin our marriage ⟶ Upset

When Gemma could accept that Paul was OK and there might be some merit in them remaining on friendly terms – rather than fighting through the courts for access to his son – she found the texts less upsetting. With the temperature in the house lowered, Paul found it easier to talk to Gemma. She could acknowledge his position and he could listen to hers. Instead of being on opposite sides, they became a team. 'In fact, these problems have brought us closer together,' Gemma said, smiling. By changing her interpretation, she had transformed her reaction:

Text $\longrightarrow$ Opportunity to bond $\longrightarrow$ Sympathy for Paul

Challenge your opinion of your partner

If, deep down, you think your partner is 'not OK', ask yourself: What is the evidence? To help challenge your interpretation put your 'evidence' to this test:

1. What is going through my mind and how much do I believe it?
2. What supports this view?
3. What contradicts my conclusions?

4. How might someone else interpret this situation?
5. What evidence is there to support alternatives?
6. What would I advise someone else to do?
7. What evidence is there to support alternative views?
8. How does my thinking help or hinder achieving my goals?
9. What effect would believing an alternative have?
10. What can I do differently?

RESPONSIBILITY PIE

For a fresh look at a particularly thorny problem between you and your partner, imagine a pie which has been divided into slices to reflect how much or how little 'responsibility' should be apportioned to each of the following:

My Partner

Myself

Family

Other People (such as an ex)

Circumstances

Greater Culture

This is what happened when Gemma did this exercise over the text messages:

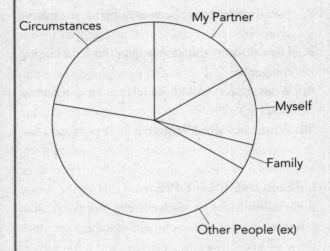

However you slice up your pie, it is always more complicated than just blaming your partner or, indeed, yourself.

Summing Up

Under stress, we can become a more exaggerated version of ourselves. Unfortunately, this encourages our partner to respond by becoming more extreme too. Although we imagine that holding on to our view is the only thing stopping our relationship from deteriorating, it is also preventing the situation from improving. By moving to a more balanced position, this will free up your partner to change too. Time and again, changing your interpretation of your partner's behaviour – from something negative to something more neutral – will change your reaction, lower the temperature in the house and make it easier to resolve the problem.

IN A NUTSHELL:

- When communication is going wrong, switch into 'Adult' mode as this will encourage your partner to do the same.
- Instead of assuming the worst, check it out. Ask your partner what he or she means rather than jumping to conclusions.
- Sometimes if you change your attitude to your partner's behaviour, it is less of a problem.

STEP 6

COMING
BACK FROM
CRISIS POINT

If there are serious problems in your relationship, it might be tempting to skip the first part of the book. However, the first five steps will lay the foundations for better communication and improve the overall atmosphere in your home. It doesn't matter if you want to persuade your partner to make major changes or simply to pick up after him- or herself, the programme works in the same way.

The big difference, at step six, is whether you have been miserable for a long time and want to bring matters to a head, or whether you were not aware of the depth of your partner's unhappiness and suddenly everything has blown up in your face. Whichever side of the crisis you stand on, whether you are about to issue an ultimatum or have just received one, it is a tough place to be and needs careful handling.

I've divided this chapter into two parts: the first section is aimed at the person initiating the crisis and the second at someone reacting to one. Please read both sections, partly for the insight into how your partner might be feeling but mainly because there are more similarities than differences between the two positions.

Initiating the Crisis

For most people the crisis has been a long time coming. Over the years, they have tried to communicate their unhappiness, boredom or frustration and although there might have been a few attempts to 'try harder', nothing has really changed. Couples can jog along in 'OK' mode for quite some time until a trigger point comes along and everything changes.

Tania, twenty-seven, had been living with her partner for eighteen months when a new arrival at work turned her life upside down. She wrote to my website: 'I'm utterly confused because no bodily fluids have been exchanged – not even a kiss. I've tried to ignore these feelings and distract myself with other projects. But I've been more fulfilled by my work colleague's written words and voice; even though I've never even shed clothes with him, I suddenly know that my partner has been going about things in the bedroom all wrong. I've avoided coming to bed until my partner's asleep and I hate being kissed by him. I feel sexy and desired on the one hand and like a duplicitous monster on the other.' Fortunately, the colleague was on only a three-week secondment to Tania's division, so she did not act on her impulses – but it was a wake-up call. 'How could I have allowed my relationship to decay to such an extent that I allowed someone else in?'

When Philippa returned home from dropping off her daughter at university – along with twenty boxes of her belongings – her heart sank: 'I walked back through the door and Michael hardly looked up from the television. I wanted to tell him about her room and how I felt waving her goodbye but he was more interested in football.' Their problems went back a long way. 'He'd always been a home-body and didn't like socialising. I'm more outgoing, except I didn't mind so much when the children were young because the house was always full of noise and activity, but over the past few years trouble had been brewing. Finally, I knew something had to change. I couldn't sit beside him on the sofa. So I turned round and went out for a walk, to clear my head, build up my courage. I had to break free or something would die inside.'

Sean's forty-second birthday party prompted his turning point: 'I've been ground down by a long commute, stress at work and home – at both places I feel taken for granted. I've been crying a lot, wanting a cuddle but not sex and, basically, my feelings have been all over the place. My wife organised this wonderful party but I just didn't want to be there.' Six months earlier Sean's father had died: 'It's a real reminder that we're not here for ever. Life's too short to be miserable or to feel this alone.'

Everybody reaches crisis point in a different way, but the impulse is the same: something must be done. Unfortunately, many people have no clear idea what that 'something' should be and little idea how to communicate effectively with their partner.

If this sounds familiar, how can you move forward? How do you explain your feelings to your partner? What if he or she is unlikely to cooperate?

Difficult people

Although I believe that 'people are OK', some partners are difficult and won't participate in solving relationship problems. In some cases, they are lost to drink, drugs or a violent temper and therefore unavailable for a relationship. Under these circumstances, you should ask yourself if it is wise to stay in this relationship.

If your relationship is fairly new – less than eighteen months old – it could be that your partner is 'OK' for someone else but not the man or woman for you (see another book in this series: *Are You Right For Me?*).

However, in the majority of cases, if your partner is 'difficult', it is because he or she is frightened and finds it harder to listen. The road ahead will be daunting but there is no reason why your relationship cannot be saved. However, it is important to find the right way of communicating. Your strategy should depend on whether your partner makes decisions based largely on intuition or rational thought.

Sensers: These are practical or rational people who are most likely to be swayed by facts and figures. They downplay emotions and favour a 'common sense' approach.

When Michael's wife, Philippa, told him she was unhappy, he couldn't understand the problem: 'You've got a lovely house, everything that you could want. No shortage of money.'

Like many Sensers, Michael concentrated on what was happening today and dismissed any past grievances. So when Philippa complained about never going out, he replied: 'But you never said anything at the time, and anyway, I can't change the past.' Logically he was right, but this only made Philippa more frustrated.

Sensers will also try to shut down an argument by concentrating on their partner's personal issues rather than accepting any problems with their relationship. Indeed, Michael told Philippa: 'I'm not stopping you going out more.'

Perhaps unsurprisingly, Philippa got angry and stormed out. However, Michael was not being difficult or dismissive. He genuinely could not understand her viewpoint, mainly because his way of processing information was entirely different.

Intuitors: These are instinctive people who are swayed more by feelings rather than argument. They are less concerned about practical matters (such as money or where to live) and more focused on abstract concepts (such as fulfilment, or being 'in love'). While Sensers are thoughtful, Intuitors speak first and think about others' reactions afterwards.

When Sean, who had a crisis after his forty-second birthday, told his wife, Madeleine, that he was unhappy and lacked direction, she exploded: 'After everything I've done, you come to me with some half-baked story. You don't love me and—'

Sean interrupted the torrent: 'I didn't say that.'

'All those years when I thought you were happy, that we were happy. All ruined.'

Intuitors tend to wrap the past into the present because, in their mind, yesterday's good times have been polluted by today's issues.

In contrast with Sensers, who take little or no responsibility for the problem, Intuitors – like Madeleine – take more than their share and often feel totally to blame.

Not surprisingly, Intuitors overreact, in stark contrast to Sensers, who downplay any problem.

What to say and what not to say

Whether your partner is a Senser or an Intuitor, please don't deliver an ultimatum. This will only create panic, start a ticking clock (where none needs to exist) and make it harder for your partner to hear your core message.

Dealing with a Senser

• Keep your explanation simple.

- Take responsibility for any personal dissatisfaction and explain what steps you are taking to remedy it.
- Explain what is making you unhappy in the relationship – placing the emphasis on today's problems.
- Avoid examples from the past, even if they illustrate the point or are connected to present issues, as your partner is likely to switch off.
- Back up your abstract goals (like more excitement) with concrete examples (like a trip to India).
- Stress value and the financial savings of your solution.
- Keep calm and don't overburden your partner by getting emotional.

Dealing with an Intuitor
- Keep your explanation simple.
- Take responsibility for any personal dissatisfaction and explain what steps you will take to remedy it.
- Tell your partner what you value about him or her.
- Explain what is making you unhappy in the relationship, being clear about when the problems started (and your happiness before that point).

- Listen to your partner and acknowledge any anger, tears or upset. Until he or she has drained their feelings, they are unlikely to be ready to truly listen.
- Keep calm.

Keep going forward

The aftermath of a confession about how unhappy you've been is always stressful and uncomfortable. The best way of dealing with the fallout, once again, depends on how your partner processes difficult situations.

If your partner is a Senser, he or she might have listened but not seemed to register the conversation. The temptation is to threaten a divorce but before you escalate matters, try writing a letter or an email. Putting your thoughts in writing gives your partner a chance to think through both your complaints and why he or she might have fallen into this trap. Here is an extract from a letter written to my website, from Desmond, prompted by his partner sending him just such an email:

I have been married for nine years and I have never been a true father, nor a husband. I've never helped around the house, cleaned up or done chores. It took my wife emailing me a detailed list of my faults for me to realise what I needed to be. I'd thought that just being here I was a better father than my dad – who divorced my mum when I was young and was never there for me – but I neglected my children to play Xbox, to go fishing or do the things I loved. I thought that because my wife didn't work, it was kind of her duty to do everything at home. I made her feel more like a maid than a wife.

In this email, she told me this was my last chance to be the husband and father she knew I could be. So I have now stepped up and started working on becoming that person. I am busting my arse off taking care of work, the kids, her, the house and anything else I can do to take some of the load off her.

So why should writing bring about such a huge change of attitude? Having read the original email to Desmond from his wife, I would make the following points. It was not too long (about eight hundred words). The tone was friendly ('I hope you had a wonderful day fishing'). It gave credit where it was due ('I'm thankful for the last nine years, you have been a great provider and allowed me the opportunity to stay home with the children' and 'Hearing "I love you" is great but you need to show us as well'). There were no threats and she did not diagnose Desmond's problems – which can get people's backs up – thereby allowing him to draw the conclusions about his father for himself. Finally, her complaints were specific and backed up with an example.

If your partner is an Intuitor, you might be tempted to back-pedal or feel overwhelmed and hopeless – but don't give up. Revealing the depth of your unhappiness will have changed the dynamics of your relationship and created a willingness to look deeper.

Malcolm and Ruth, both in their early fifties, had been living together for nearly thirty years and had a child together but they had not got married. Although there had been good times, Ruth had not felt truly loved over the past five years. When she initiated the crisis that brought them into counselling, she told Malcolm: 'I have never felt sure of you – right from the beginning you could not commit to me. I sort of understood because I'd come out of a long-term relationship and didn't want to fall in love either.' They had been students on an overland bus exploring Europe and Asia. 'But I couldn't understand why you shut me out and wanted to go off sightseeing with the others,' she continued, 'because I loved you so much and always wanted to be with you.'

It was Malcolm's turn to speak: 'You keep using your overwhelming love as an excuse for being demanding. You can't see that it's like a form of abuse. You stop me from going off and doing the things that interest me.' They were already well aware of the pattern of Ruth clasping Malcolm tight and him wriggling away. However, Ruth's declaration that they should sort this problem out or call it a day provided the focus to start facing the central 'unsayable' issue in their relationship – how to balance individual space and couple togetherness – and finally begin to resolve it.

Whether your partner is a Senser or an Intuitor, it is worth remembering the lessons of the last chapter and valuing the benefits of how your partner approaches a problem. A good decision needs the cool head of the Senser (who weighs up all the evidence) *and* the emotional intelligence of the Intuitor (who listens to any messages from the unconscious). If you can work together to solve your relationship's underlying problems, you have the makings of a good team.

Finally, if you have been suppressing the seriousness of your relationship problems for quite some time, it is likely that you will be feeling depressed. The following exercise will help you find enough energy to keep going forward.

BEAT THE BLUES

The blues kick in whenever we feel overwhelmed by helplessness. This is why even something very minor, but empowering, can help us break out.

- Set up small triumphs and easy successes. For example, tackling a nasty chore that you have delayed for ages – such as sorting out the cupboard under the sink. Afterwards these jobs will provide a real sense of achievement.
- Find small boosts to your self-image. At the weekend, make certain that you get dressed rather than slobbing round in your dressing gown or splash out on some new clothes.
- Help other people. Offering to fix the guttering for an elderly neighbour or volunteering for the Girl Guides' camp will not only divert your attention from your own problems but their thanks will make you feel better about yourself.
- Compare yourself to someone worse off. Cancer patients often reassure themselves by comparing themselves to someone sicker. Next time you find yourself wishing your life was like that of a lucky friend, try being thankful it is not like someone much less fortunate than you.
- Take up some exercise as the endorphins lift spirits, help relaxation and take your mind off worries.

- If you are religious, try praying; if not, look for a meditation class. These are often run by local Buddhist centres. They will not look to convert you but rather teach you to empty your mind. It is a hard goal but even getting a few moments peace from an overactive brain can be very uplifting.

How to Get Your Lover Back

If your partner has dropped the bombshell that he or she is seriously unhappy or is threatening to break up your relationship, you will probably still be reeling from the shock. So try not to panic, make a snap decision or expect to solve the problems overnight. It will take time and contemplation, but the following advice will significantly improve your chances of success.

Acknowledge your partner's message

Your partner will probably say some shocking and hurtful things. It is natural to want to defend yourself or put the record straight. However, this will probably prompt a row, sound like you are making excuses, and prevent your partner from recognising that you have truly heard him or her.

Instead, acknowledge your partner's message by repeating back the key items. For example: 'You've been unhappy for years and feel taken for granted.' (Don't worry if you are stressed and might not have heard everything properly, your partner will clarify, for example, 'not "taken for granted" but ignored'.)

Keep asking questions, so you can be sure that you have properly understood. From time to time, summarise your partner's case back to him or her. This will help you check that you are neither downplaying nor exaggerating the situation.

Finally, when your partner is all talked out and feels heard – ask, if you're unsure – you can explain your position and feelings.

Acknowledge your failings

Although it is tempting to present yourself in the best light possible, accepting justified criticism will build a rapport between you and your partner. It also shows that you have truly listened, that you accept there are problems in the relationship, and that you take your share of responsibility for what's gone wrong. Most importantly, acknowledging your failings will help build trust.

Kip Williams, a psychologist at the University of Toledo in Ohio, studied what happened when lawyers exposed a weakness in their case before the other team had a chance to point it out. Interestingly, the jurors rated the lawyers who confessed their failings as more trustworthy and therefore listened more carefully to their case.

To increase the power of this strategy, be specific. I often counsel people trying to save their marriage, who tell their partner: 'I know I'm not perfect.' Unfortunately, this sort of blanket acknowledgement seldom works as it fails to show an understanding of how their behaviour impacted on their partner. A more effective approach would be: 'I know I should have listened more' or 'I should have tried harder'.

So think about what you would like to do differently and talk over your findings with your partner.

Take responsibility for your failings

We imagine that blaming our problems on circumstances beyond our control will get us an easier ride. However, research suggests that it is best to own up and take responsibility.

Social scientist Fiona Lee studied the results of public-listed companies and found that those where company chairmen put the blame on something internal (and therefore under their control) rather than external (like the global market, weather or economy) had higher stock prices one year later. Why should this be? Lee believes that companies that took responsibility were considered by stockholders to have diagnosed the problems and were attending to them. Meanwhile, the companies that blamed forces out of their control appeared helpless and hapless.

So how do you use this research? Instead of blaming 'pressure of work' or 'the children eating up all the time' – which are external problems – take responsibility: 'I didn't prioritise home life' or 'I need to make certain we can have time away together.' This will show your partner that you're willing to act as a team to resolve the underlying problems.

Finally, use this strategy sparingly. Don't go overboard and take all the responsibility for the crisis; good communication is a joint responsibility. In addition, one or two failings build trust; a long list sounds hopeless.

Get a personal recommendation

On the one hand, you don't want to talk about your strengths, achievements and the goodness of your character as this would sound boastful.

Yet, on the other hand, it is important to remind your partner that although the relationship might appear broken, you still have many positive qualities.

Get round this quandary by asking someone close to you to sing your praises. It does not matter if the personal recommendation comes from your mother – who is bound to praise – or another member of your family.

However, don't involve your children as you don't want to alarm them. The other warning is to use this strategy sparingly. One recommendation reminds your partner of your good qualities. Several can sound like an attempt at brainwashing and turn him or her off.

Collaborate

When it comes to solving a crisis, many heads are better than one. However, think through whom you will recruit to help. Although it is nice to have people cheering you on, someone who can see both sides of the argument, or who is willing to point out where you are going wrong, is far more valuable. So look for a team who can offer support, a sounding board and knowledge of the road ahead.

The good news is that, by reading this book, you've already embraced the importance of collaborating. So let's look back over what you have learned and how specifically to harness the programme to your needs. Step one – 'Stop What Doesn't Work' – is particularly important. When you are stressed, you are likely to fall back into old habits. Be doubly resolved to avoid this trap as it will confirm your partner's fears that change is impossible. Unlike many people reading this book – who are dealing with smaller, day-to-day issues – you will also need to make big changes to kick-start the healing process and to address your partner's need for change. However, don't overlook steps two and three – 'Do Less' and 'Think Smarter' – as smaller changes will show a depth to your determination and a willingness to revolutionise your relationship.

If you are seeking to nudge your partner into giving your relationship a second chance, the next exercise is particularly effective.

LABELLING

We are always assigning traits, attitudes, beliefs and labels to other people. This is why airlines use announcements on arrival like: 'We know you have many airlines to choose from, so we thank you for choosing to fly with us.' It sends all sorts of subtle messages. First, the announcement reminds you that you have chosen them. Second, it confirms your confidence in your choice – after all, you've landed safely and on time. Without any cost, and minimum effort, they have labelled themselves as a great company. How can you use this knowledge to persuade your partner?

- **Check the labels that you are giving your partner.** Continually and anxiously asking your partner 'How are you feeling?', 'Any changes?', 'Should we talk about our situation?' just labels the relationship as 'in crisis'. Worse still, by labelling your partner as someone 'about to leave', you could turn your fears into a self-fulfilling prophesy.

- **Give your partner a positive label.** Alternatives include: 'You're a reasonable person', 'We've always tried to make decisions together' or 'I know you don't want to hurt me.' Obviously these have to come from the heart and be genuinely credible, so your partner recognises him- or herself.

- **Make a request in keeping with this label.** For example, 'I know you don't want to hurt me, so I'd be grateful if you could come to counselling with me' or 'You're a reasonable person, so I hope you'll tell me if . . .'

Dealing With Criticism, Rejection and Setbacks

In an ideal world, your partner will notice your determination to change and support the process. Unfortunately, he or she will be angry or fed up after years of working alone on the relationship and therefore highly sceptical. So instead of co-operation, you are likely to face obstacles and stonewalling, but don't despair. Here are the most common problems, the possible pitfalls and some effective fight-back strategies:

'My partner is not only critical but sometimes downright nasty'

It is tough enough dealing with a negative partner but quite another thing to deal with someone whose criticism has become personal.

After spending seven years together and having two children, Edward and Adrienne had hit a wall in their marriage. Adrienne complained that there was no 'connection' between them and was adamant that they should split. She agreed to come to counselling only because Edward begged. When I asked how things had been at home, Edward complained that Adrienne's behaviour towards him had been 'horrible, bordering on hate and a lot of resentment'. He was puzzled and unable to understand why trying to save his marriage should be greeted with such a response.

However, there are always two sides to an argument. Adrienne sat in the chair opposite silently fuming. So I asked Edward if he had done anything to justify this reaction? 'I'd taken the kids for a weekend away – it had originally been planned as a break for me and Adrienne, but she refused to come, so my mum came instead. We all had a wonderful time together, although I had an empty ache inside, but I did my best to ignore it. When we returned all happy, Adrienne said something that triggered something inside me and I flew off the handle and shouted at her and said hurtful things for which I later apologised.'

Adrienne finally spoke: 'Tell him what you called me.'

Edward shook his head.

'He called me a "bitch" and a whole lot worse. He says he loves me, he wants to make the relationship work and that's how he behaves.'

'That was completely wrong and I did apologise.' Edward obviously imagined that this wiped the slate clean.

Meanwhile, Adrienne sank back into silence.

Worst mistake: Fighting fire with fire. However much you feel justified in losing your temper and ranting, your partner will just view your outburst as proof that the relationship is fundamentally flawed.

Fight-back strategy: Acknowledge your partner's feelings – for example, 'I can see that you're angry.' Although this might encourage your partner to off-load – which could be unpleasant – it is better than trying to dam or divert his or her feelings. However much you are provoked by what you hear, keep calm and then report your own feelings.

'Nothing I do seems to make any difference'

When your partner unilaterally declares that your marriage is over, the pain is overwhelming. One half of your brain can't believe it's happening and the other is trying to fix the mess as quickly as possible. It is almost as if you're looking for a magic solution to make everything all right again.

'I stumbled across a photo of us both looking happy from last summer,' said Edward on his first solo counselling session – Adrienne had refused to continue. 'So I had this idea and put together a mini-album of good moments and a letter, not asking her to stay, but explaining how I feel, and posted them to her with a CD of two songs that I sang on. I hope it will be a pleasant surprise and she doesn't see it as desperate, and that they evoke some emotion in her like they did in me. I suspect it will have the opposite effect, but I am running out of options.'

Worst mistake: Becoming so fixated on your magic solution that you're blind to the bigger picture. Meanwhile your partner cannot understand why, when the marital ship is sinking, you are so preoccupied with rearranging the deck chairs. When your efforts such as going for one counselling session, arranging a romantic trip to Paris or spending a family Christmas together don't have the desired effect, the likelihood is that you will explode or sink into depression.

Fight-back strategy: When people claim to have tried everything, what they mean is that they've tried every ingenious trick to 'magic' their marriage back to health. However, they have not tried listening to their partner – truly listening. By this, I mean imagining that everything your partner says is true (just for a minute) and imagining how he or she must be feeling. Standing in your partner's shoes, however temporarily, will help you begin to address the real issues.

'My partner is shutting down his or her feelings'

After the initial declaration that a relationship is in crisis, couples do a lot of talking. Often these discussions go round in circles – normally because each partner has diametrically opposed opinions. There might be the occasional optimistic sign – like the initiator buys flowers – but slowly the mood becomes darker until communication grinds to a halt. So what's going on? There are three possible scenarios.

First, the initiator feels it is pointless trying to explain any more because his or her partner will never 'get it'. This could be because he or she is too upset to hear, contradicts everything, or simply shouts down all opposition.

Second, the initiator finds it hard to understand the situation him- or herself; he or she is fed up with going through the daily motions and wants more out of life, but can't really explain what. In most cases, the initiator is going through some form of mid-life crisis or sliding into depression.

Finally, the initiator is keeping something back. When Edward finally learned to listen to Adrienne, she admitted that she'd been speaking to an old flame behind his back. 'She says she has feelings for him but she doesn't know what those feelings are,' he explained at his third solo session. Sometimes there is a full-blown affair, but normally a friend or work colleague is becoming more than 'just a good friend'. Edward was in despair: 'Why didn't she tell me?' The initiator can be simply ashamed of his or her behaviour. However, more often, they consider the 'friendship' to be a side issue (a symptom of the problem not the cause) but suspect their partner will zero in on this other person and blame everything on them.

Worst mistake: Thinking it will all blow over. When everything goes quiet, or the initiator stops complaining, the partner trying to save the relation-ship manages to convince him- or herself that things are getting better. On the surface this might be true, but the initiator is either preparing their exit or distracting themselves with a self-medication affair.

Fight-back strategy: Sometimes things have to get worse to get better. Although the truth might hurt, at least all the problems are in the open and can finally be addressed. Keep calm and don't be distracted from the real issues.

'I feel like I'm wasting my time'

Once you have reached this scenario, the situation is indeed bleak. Your partner is no longer spiteful or nasty – which should make you feel better – but being ignored or being seen as irrelevant is worse. The hours spent going round and round the same old subjects was draining and depressing, but at least you were talking.

When Edward arrived for his fourth session, he sounded defeated, deflated and dejected. 'I persuaded her to explain what she wants from life and she listed five things – own her own house, have a stable family life for the children, have a career when the children start school, be in a loving, happy relationship and I can't remember the fifth. But she can have those things now and all the freedom she desires. Yet if we split, we both will be on the breadline for the foreseeable future; she admitted that it will set her back five to ten years.' He took his head out of his hands. 'I feel we do have the "loving, happy relationship", but she says we don't have the emotional connection and the physical relationship. Our relationship is deeper than that and we have many, many other important connections – like the children. Yet she seems hell-bent on achieving this fairy-tale love.' It was a classic sense-versus-intuitive debate but instead of engaging with the arguments on a deeper level, Edward was about to throw in the towel. He had not stopped loving his wife but wondered if giving up, attempting to switch off his feelings or 'seeing other people' would make him feel better.

Worst mistake: Begging for another chance or making empty promises. This is not only a sure sign that you have not been listening to your partner – even though he or she has been trying to communicate in increasingly negative ways – but also offers no plausible vision of how your relationship could improve. Worse still, begging destroys your self-esteem and forfeits any lingering respect from your partner.

Fight-back strategy: Instead of waiting for a sign that the relationship is 'not beyond hope' or pushing for an agreement to 'try again', take the initiative and start working on the relationship yourself. Understand what went wrong, think about the changes you'd like to make, and start to implement them. Who is most likely to spark your partner's interest again: someone getting on with their life and doing interesting things or someone mired in bitterness and forever bringing up old grievances?

What Do I Really Want?

Whether you are the person initiating a crisis or the person reacting to one, it is important to have a clear idea of your goal. It will give you something to cling on to during the difficult weeks ahead and improve communication with your partner. Unfortunately, many people find it hard to articulate what they want.

Paula, from the last chapter, whose husband was unhappy but couldn't decide whether he wanted to stay and work on the relationship or leave, found this task particularly difficult: 'But it's not what I want, everything is down to Jeff. I'm just waiting for him to make his mind up.'

'Except that there are two of you in this relationship,' I replied, 'and what you want has to count too. Imagine that I have a magic wand under my chair, what would you wish for?'

Paula was silent.

'It's a magic wand, so you can have *anything*.'

Finally she replied: 'I want him to love me back.'

I wrote her statement on a flip-chart in large letters, as writing down a key goal not only makes it more real but also fixes it in the front of our mind. There were tears in Paula's eyes. 'Why was that so hard to say?' I asked.

'I don't want to be rejected again.'

Like many people in her situation, Paula was fighting for her marriage with one hand but holding back with the other – frightened of getting hurt. Not only did this behaviour cut her firepower by half, but it also sent out a mixed message. Paula immediately recognised this trap.

'One moment, I'm telling him he doesn't have to sleep on the sofa and inviting him to bed and making love, but the next I'm angry and sending him back downstairs.'

'And what would happen if he did reject you?' I asked.

'I would just have to get on with it,' she said. This time, there were no tears or upset – just total calmness.

In effect, Paula had looked calmly at her greatest fear and knew that if the worst came to the worst, she could cope. She left the session feeling not only better but also more in charge of her future.

Although it might seem dangerous to admit out loud what you want, I believe it is always best to fight for your heart's desire and lose than to give up without a struggle. So if you are coping with the fallout from your partner's declaration of unhappiness, don't wait for a sign or some encour-agement from him or her to make your wish come true. Write it down and turn it into your mission statement through the difficult months ahead.

At first sight, the partner initiating the crisis should find it easier to explain their goal. Unfortunately, it often comes out as what they *don't* want rather than what they *do*. When I asked Sean, whose crisis started at his forty-second birthday party, for his goals, he replied: 'I don't want to be like my father, always doing what other people expect' and 'to break out of this rut'. Knowing what he wished to avoid was fine but it did not bring Sean any closer to changing his life. When I asked him to imagine a magic wand, he said: 'I want to travel' and 'I want more responsibility at work'. By framing his goal as a positive, rather than a negative, he could immediately think of some steps to turn his dream into a reality.

Whichever side of the crisis divide you're standing on, there is one word that will make it easier to communicate your goal to your partner. This word is *because*. There are two reasons why 'because' is so powerful: it explains and it contains.

Taking Paula as an example, she told Jeff: 'I want you to love me back *because* through all this upheaval I've discovered the depth of my feelings for you. Beforehand, I'd really just been going through the motions.' She had explained why she wanted the relationship to continue and contained Jeff's imagination by heading off any possible alternative conclusions – like wanting to stay together for the sake of the children, saving money or keeping up appearances.

In Sean's case, he told Madeleine: 'I want to travel *because* I never got the chance when I was younger. I went off to university and got stuck into a job.' This explained his feeling of missing out but contained Madeleine's fears – for example, that he wanted to get away from her.

THE 'RIGHT TRAP'

When a couple is in conflict, and the arguments get nasty, both partners are quick to cloak themselves in righteousness. However, 'being right' is a trap. It casts your partner as 'wrong', part of the problem and therefore 'deserving' of your anger, bitterness and frustration. Worse still, your partner is defending his or her unpleasant behaviour by using the same defence of being 'right'. So break this destructive cycle by using the following exercise:

* After a row, instead of pumping up your anger by going over all the points where you were in the 'right' and your partner was in the 'wrong', close your eyes and imagine that you are

walking through the jungle when the ground suddenly gives way.

- You have fallen into the 'Right Trap' – a deep, dark pit which has been camouflaged by a few innocent-looking sticks (day-to-day issues) which don't seem threatening but easily break.
- Imagine looking round the pit, in your mind, and think about all the things that you have been 'right' about: how might your partner think he or she is 'right' on those issues too?
- If you cannot imagine your partner being 'right' about these specific circumstances, pan back – like a camera – and reveal more of the past days, months and years: are there reasons from your wider life together why she or he might feel 'right' on this issue?
- Ask yourself: Is being right getting me anywhere?
- Ultimately, there is your 'right' and your partner's 'right' and, probably, if a hundred different people were polled on the same circumstances, they would come up with countless more 'rights'.
- So climb out of the 'Right Trap' by no longer discussing your marital problems with friends – who will side with you and reinforce your belief that your interpretation is the only 'right' one.

- Finally, imagine standing outside the 'Right Trap' and feeling how good it is to be up in the light again, able to see your partner's viewpoint too.

Moving Forward

Whether you are the person who has initiated the crisis or the person reacting to one, if you have acknowledged your partner's feelings, truly listened and accepted that there need to be changes, the atmosphere should be much more positive. But how do you keep building on these changes?

Concentrate on how far you've come

It is easy to be daunted by the scale of the task of rescuing your relationship. So look at what you have achieved already – especially as the first steps are the hardest – rather than what still needs to be done. Strangely enough, the last part of the journey will be the most straightforward. This is because the closer we are to achieving our goal, the more confident we feel and therefore the harder we push to achieve it.

Focus on the changes you'd like

When things are going badly, it is nearly always because one or both of you have slipped back into old ways and either stopped communicating effectively or communicated only negatives. So refocus on what works and find positive short-term goals to make your relationship better.

Give yourself time

In the same way that a relationship deteriorates slowly over months and years of disappointment, it takes time to rebuild trust again. So don't expect results too quickly; both parties will need solid evidence that any changes are lasting and that the gains will not slip away. Ultimately, you will need both *patience* and *persistence*.

I often see people who possess just one of these qualities but not the other. Persistence alone is a problem as it can easily become demanding, anxious and dissatisfied. Patience alone is also a problem. The risk is that nothing changes or someone minimises their own needs and always puts others' first – until they become resentful and angry. However, the golden combination of patience and persistence is nearly always rewarded with a greatly improved relationship.

The Long Picture

Sometimes the odds are so stacked against a relationship that separation is the only answer. However, a temporary split does not necessarily have to become permanent. Christine's forty-seven-year-old husband announced that he had fallen in love at a distance with a colleague (who was almost oblivious to his feelings), bought a flat and threatened to move in. At that point, Christine had little hope and felt 'sick with misery'.

Her husband did leave but when nothing happened with his colleague, not even a kiss, he started a passionate affair with a second colleague that lasted around four months. Despite her hurt, Christine kept the lines of communication open: 'Throughout the year, he has been visiting me and our daughters (now ten and twelve) every second weekend, or usually more frequently, and stays over in the spare room. He phones nightly to speak to the children but he always talks to me too.'

One year after the split, there seemed to be a window of opportunity to try again after Christine's husband split with his girlfriend: 'We have a lot to talk about in the sense of books, films, gossip and other mutual interests. We have lots of laughs and give each other a kiss and hug good night. I certainly have to have this affectionate connection because if it wasn't there, my feelings would soon turn to total resentment and hate.'

Christine had used the time apart to take up her profession again, get individual counselling and work on herself: 'I no longer have any cause to moan boringly about work and in public am pretty much the happy and feisty person I was when we met twenty-three years ago – except for being lovelorn, sad and angry when alone. My friends admire my generosity and say "hang on in there". Could we find our relationship again or is it just fantasy?'

As in many cases where the relationship was basically sound but suddenly imploded, Christine's husband seemed to have suffered some form of midlife crisis – where everything in his old life no longer made sense and escape into a fantasy relationship seemed the only solution. Once someone in this situation has calmed down, taken stock and realised that an exploratory affair has made their life worse rather than better, there is nearly always a chance to try again. (See *How Can I Ever Trust You Again?* for more information about affairs and how they self-destruct.)

If there is a window of opportunity for a second chance, how can you seize the moment? First of all, avoid talking about 'The Future' as this will sound like an immensely scary project. Instead, discuss 'going on a few dates' or 'getting to know each other again'.

Your partner will be worried about 'leading you on' or 'hurting you again'. So bring these fears into the open and let him or her talk. However, stress that you are an adult and take responsibility for your own feelings and choices. Your partner does not need to 'protect' you. You are an adult going into this with your eyes open – not a child that's been promised a pony!

Christine's husband was indeed worried and told her: 'I don't know if I can have sex with you again.' I helped her keep both his and her anxiety down by framing everything over the next few days. So Christine told him: 'I'm only asking if you fancy going to the movies, not inviting you into my bed.'

Many partners who are considering returning are worried about 'spoiling the friendship'. If this is the case, I think it is important to be honest and tell your partner that you will be upset in the short term but your number one priority will remain being the best possible parent for your children (and how that means still cooperating with each other).

Coping during the long picture

If you and your partner are currently having 'time apart' and you're considering playing the long game, it is important to focus on the following:

- Work on yourself and healing your pain (rather than relying on your partner to return and make everything better).
- Keep the children out of your marital problems. Although it will be hard, protect them from the worst of your pain or they will feel duty-bound to side with you.
- Step back and stop analysing. Don't try to second-guess the meaning behind your partner's behaviour or ask friends for reports of his or her feelings. Someone in crisis can experience everything from euphoria to despair in one day, so even if you do guess the correct feeling, another will be along shortly.
- Understand what went wrong and what changes need to be made (either for trying again with your partner or for avoiding making the same mistakes with someone new).
- Review at six months and a year.

Summing Up

Whichever side of the crisis divide you are standing on, remove any 'ticking clock' – a sense that everything must be sorted immediately. Understand why communication has been a problem and whether you put more stress on rational thought (Senser) or feelings (Intuitor). Check you are giving a clear message to your partner and don't expect a result overnight.

IN A NUTSHELL:

- Think clearly about your main goal and how to communicate it consistently. Make certain that your words and actions match.
- Put yourself in your partner's shoes and try seeing the situation from his or her position.
- Instead of trying to second-guess your partner's state of mind, try asking a direct question about his or her feelings.

STEP 7

NO TURNING BACK

Following the previous steps will have significantly improved your relationship and made cooperation a normal part of your relationship rather than a special favour. However, to cement these changes in place, you need to adopt six helpful habits or ways of looking at your relationship.

Understand Your Pattern

Instead of trying to post-mortem individual rows or disagreements, take a step back and look at the patterns. If you can understand this bigger picture, you can head off unnecessary arguments and focus your attention on solving the sources of long-running disputes. So look at the following exercises; the idea is to understand just how closely your actions and those of your partner are linked, so try and find as many examples as possible.

IN THE RUN-UP TO AN ARGUMENT

When my partner does:
a) ....
b) ....
c) ....

I tend to:
a) ....
b) ....
c) ....

When I:
a) ....
b) ....
c) ....

My partner tends to:
a) ....
b) ....
c) ....

When I did this exercise with Megan, twenty-five, and Harvey, twenty-nine, she immediately put: 'When Harvey goes all quiet, I tend to get anxious and worried.'

'What else?' I asked.

'When Harvey is still quiet, I push and push until I lose my temper and shout.'

If I had been working with Megan alone, she would have filled in what Harvey did in these two circumstances, but as Harvey was there I asked him. 'When Megan loses her temper, I keep quiet so I don't make things worse,' he replied.

'What else?' I asked.

'When I walk away, that makes her angrier and angrier,' he confessed.

Like in the famous argument about which came first, the chicken or the egg, it does not matter whether Megan's temper made Harvey withdraw or Harvey's silence made Megan angry.

Ultimately, arguments are not your fault or your partner's but the combination of the two of you.

The next exercise looks at our expectations of our partner – these are the hundreds of small services, attributes or reactions that we require our partner to observe or possess – but in most cases, we have never spoken out loud.

ON A DAY-TO-DAY BASIS

What I expect from my partner ....

....

Why? ....

....

| Is it fair? ....
| ....
|
| Could I do this myself? ....
| ....

One of the sources of rows between Megan and Harvey was DIY and household maintenance tasks. So when Megan did this exercise, she wrote down: 'I expect my partner to fix things.' She had never really thought why she expected this. However, when we looked at her childhood, her memories of her father seemed always to feature him with a toolbox in hand. Megan stopped for a second: 'I just thought that if Harvey really cared, he'd make an effort.'

'But is that fair?'

'Not really, he's not interested or particularly handy and just because my dad did it, why should he?' Megan conceded.

Finally, we looked at the alternatives to arguing about DIY. Megan could start fixing stuff herself (perhaps after some lessons from her dad) or pay someone else to do the job.

ME AND MY SHADOW

Every family has its rules. Some of them are very explicit: 'Wash your hands before sitting down at the table' or 'Don't talk with your mouth full'. The really important rules, however, are seldom stated directly but policed by disapproving looks, ominous silences, sarcastic put-downs and ostracism. So we learn from an early age that some feelings, behaviour or desires are simply unacceptable. Because we want to be loved by our parents, grandparents, brothers and sisters, we play along and try to follow the rules. Unfortunately, these 'unacceptable' parts of our character do not simply disappear – because they are part of being human – so we suppress or hide them away. In many ways, they are our shadow – very much part of us but simply unacknowledged.

Here are some of these rules: Don't fail, Don't get above yourself, Don't be such a child, Don't grow up, Don't make too much fuss, Don't feel, Don't get angry, Don't be cleverer than me, Stop putting yourself first.

Sometimes the rules are expressed in an open, positive way. For example, 'You're the pretty one' or 'You're the brains' or 'You're so helpful'. However, there is an unspoken downside to this:

you have to be pretty, brainy or helpful to be loved. Meanwhile, the contrasting parts of your personality (sporty, frivolous or irresponsible) disappear into the shadows.

So ask yourself the following questions:

1. What were the unspoken rules when I was growing up?

2. What were the taboo feelings?

3. What did I miss out on by keeping those parts of myself in the dark?

4. What impact has it had on my relationship?

5. What would happen if I brought my shadow out into the light?

6. What is my worst fear? (Try and be as explicit as possible.)

7. How likely is this to happen?

Focus on More Fun Together

When I listen to many couples talk about their evenings and weekends together, it sounds like a round of jobs to be completed, children to be ferried around and other obligations to be fulfilled. 'I just can't settle if there are clothes in the drier that should be folded or the kitchen tops haven't been wiped down,' said Hilary, thirty-three. She was often exhausted and complained that her husband, Tony, forty-five, didn't do enough to help: 'He's always saying "Put that down" or "It can wait" and wanting me to relax and watch television with him, which would be nice, but has he ever thought that I wouldn't be rushing around so much if he did his share?' We could have spent weeks negotiating what tasks, when and how, but I sensed the issue was deeper. It was almost as if Hilary had a heavy heart and although more support might have helped, it would never be enough to lighten her load.

So I tried a different approach: 'What do you do for fun?' They looked blank and it took about twenty seconds for either of them to respond. I felt like I'd asked for directions to the moon. Finally Hilary answered:

'We have friends round from time to time.'

But Tony interrupted: 'Not for a long time.'

'I go over to my sister's and we share a bottle of wine.'

'I have an old school friend down in Devon and I go down there once a month for the fishing.'

No wonder everything felt so heavy. Life was a round of work, chores and getting by. There was no chance to relax, be carefree and have the sort of fun that leaves you feeling light-headed and giggly. So we focused on them having more fun together, rather than on more housework. The next week, the atmosphere in the room had been transformed.

'It was a lovely autumn day and rather than working in the garden, we decided to go for a walk in the local country park,' said Tony.

'I don't know what came over me, but he was off in a world of his own and I sneaked behind a tree and jumped out at him.'

'Gave me the fright of my life.'

'And you chased me and we kicked this pile of leaves at each other.'

'Much better than raking them up at home.'

'And we dammed that stream with sticks and fallen leaves.'

'I hadn't done that since I was twelve,' said Tony.

'When we returned home, Tony offered to make tea and I sat down and read the paper.'

With plenty of goodwill floating around, Hilary didn't need to ask for help because Tony had already offered. If you'd like to bring more fun into your relationship, follow these simple guidelines:

- **Differentiate between urgent and important.** (The leaves in Tony and Hilary's garden did need to be raked up at some point, but it was not *urgent* and therefore did not need to take precedence over everything else.)
- **Set aside plenty of relaxing time together.** (Intimacy and fun cannot just be ordered up. Tony and Hilary needed unstructured time in the park to relax and reconnect before they could let go and indulge themselves.)
- **Don't be afraid to play.** (Private jokes and anything that leaves you breathless, sweaty and dirty are almost guaranteed to bring out your inner child.)
- **You can be happy together, even if you can't solve all your problems.** (Hilary and Tony still needed to work on many other areas but having the right mindset had transformed their relationship.)

GENERATE EVEN MORE GOODWILL

Here are five proven ways for increasing goodwill in your partner. Try doing one a day and you'll keep the marital therapist away!

- Respond cheerfully to your partner's request.
- Look for something that needs to be done and do it without being asked.
- Give your partner a cuddle or a hug (without expecting it to lead to sex).
- Come home with an unexpected small gift.
- Compliment your partner in front of other people. (For example, 'He is very generous' or 'I admire how elegant she looks.')

Look for the Third Way

The third way is another idea from politics and came out of former president Bill Clinton's attempt to position himself above the simple right/left split that had dominated politics since the Second World War, and to co-opt the best from each world view. So how does it work for loving relationships? If you relax the urgency of your own case and develop empathy for your partner's viewpoint, the atmosphere in the house is immediately depolarised. Out of the calmness, something wonderful emerges. It will take a little time, so don't expect an immediate result, but a third option (not your way and not your partner's way) will slowly emerge.

Margery had expected her husband, Gregory, to retire at sixty (as his company had a policy of not putting more money into staff pension pots at this age). However, Gregory found his work rewarding and his employers were keen to retain his services. 'I've always played second fiddle to that damn company,' said Margery bitterly. 'I've dropped my career and followed him round the world and I thought this would finally be our time.'

Gregory saw things differently: 'I have a team and we're working on this big account at the moment and I can't let them down, and, anyway, I don't feel ready to retire.'

'That's all well and good but I'm left twiddling my thumbs rather than enjoying doing things together.'

They both had a valid case. So I decided to use the third way and see if another option beyond retirement or continuing working would emerge:

- **Express empathy for each other's position.** Margery said: 'I know you've always got a lot of satisfaction and your identity from your work.' Gregory said: 'We have great fun together; I want to spend time with you.'

- **State as objectively as possible your needs and why you feel like that.** Margery said: 'I want some project or plan for our retirement.' Meanwhile Gregory said: 'I have ambitions and responsibilities at work. I don't feel ready for slippers.'

- **What do you accept about your partner's position?** (Remember, you don't have to be in wholehearted agreement.) Margery said: 'I share your need for something more than slippers.' Gregory said: 'I would like to buy a house abroad and do it up together.'

- **What small step could you make to show goodwill and go some way to alleviating the situation?** The couple agreed to plan their weekends and holidays – rather than Gregory just flopping around the house and unwinding from work – and started researching possible places to buy a second home.

- **Sit back and wait.** Margery looked into a second career – something interesting but which would not tie her to nine-to-five. Eventually, she decided to train as a magistrate.

Gregory enjoyed their weekends so much, he negotiated an extra day off every fortnight with his employers. Finally, instead of seeing their two positions as incompatible, Margery and Gregory began to understand how they could be complementary: they could both relax and enjoy life, plus seek new challenges.

SWAP-OVER WEEKEND

To help you truly empathise with your partner, and help facilitate your own third way, why not try this idea:

- To gain a fresh insight into what it is like to be your partner, you take over his or her jobs for the weekend.
- Meanwhile, your partner takes on your role.
- So if you normally take the children swimming, your partner will do that task. If he or she cuts the grass or does the supermarket shop, then you take over.
- Try and recreate each other's weekends as much as possible. The more you swap, the greater the understanding.
- Look for things you take for granted and that are so second nature that you have never questioned them before – for example, who is responsible for initiating sex.

- At the end of the weekend, relax and talk about your experiences of being each other, the insights gained and what you might do differently in the future.

Accept What You Can't Change

A musical comedy ran in New York at the end of the nineties for over five thousand performances, and was subsequently performed all over the world; a lot of its success was down to its witty title: *I Love You, You're Perfect, Now Change.* Audiences responded so warmly because they immediately recognised the absurd truth about love. On the one hand, we love our partner just the way he or she is, but on the other, we'd love him or her a little bit more if only he'd or she'd . . . (fill in your particular bugbear).

When Jessica brought Gary into counselling, her main complaint was about his moods: 'He'll arrive home with such a long face that it pulls me right down.' Gary was equally unhappy: 'She's on my case all the time, "Would I like this?", "What's the matter?" or "Cheer up, it'll never happen".'

The situation had got worse since they had started a family and Jessica would pester Gary to play with his son: 'I want Gary to get the best out of him.' Jessica's motives might have been good but it was driving a wedge between them. It also sounded like she was *coaching* Gary. I wondered what message that might be giving him. Jessica looked thoughtful but before she could answer, Gary chipped in:

'You're not quite good enough the way you are.'

'How does that make you feel?' I asked.

'Unloved,' he replied.

But what would happen if Jessica reframed her attitude to Gary's 'moods' not as a *problem* but as a *fact of life?* (After all, Gary had often said: 'I'm not always down, I just have one of those faces.') This is because a 'problem', invites a solution. Whereas a 'fact of life' – like some people are naturally more pessimistic – is something that has to be accommodated.

Jessica agreed to see what would happen if she stopped trying to manage Gary's moods and his relationship with their son. First of all, the atmosphere in the house lightened – as they were having fewer rows. Jessica admitted: 'It was hard to hold back. I thought nothing would change if I didn't do something, but actually I'm not responsible for his feelings – only he can be.' Second, Gary started playing more with his son: 'I could join in when it felt right – like when he wanted help with building a tower out of his bricks – rather than barging in.'

By accepting what she couldn't change, Jessica had not only accepted Gary (in all his complexity) but also allowed him to have a different attitude to bringing up children. Their son could also fully benefit from their differences. Jessica could be a proactive mother – and head off any potential problems – and Gary could stand back and give their son enough space to learn things for himself. There is another benefit. We need difference to keep love and sexual attraction, otherwise there is a danger of becoming so alike – almost brother and sister – that all desire disappears. (There is more in my book *I Love You But I'm Not In Love With You*.)

Another example of reframing a 'problem' as a 'fact of life' is Maxine and Rosie – a lesbian couple in their thirties. Maxine wanted Rosie to give up smoking: 'I hate the smell, what it does to her health and, when we're out shopping, if we stop for a coffee I have to sit outside in the cold if I want to talk to Rosie,' said Maxine. She tried complaining, bribing and persuading Rosie to cut down by rolling her own – all without success. In fact, she had tried everything other than accepting that she couldn't change Rosie. It was hard not to drop hints, sigh or get stroppy when Rosie slipped out for a cigarette, though slowly but surely she accepted Rosie's smoking as a 'fact of life'. 'She'd smoked when I first met her, so it's not like I didn't know – I just thought I could change her,' Maxine said, laughing.

Interestingly, twelve months later, Rosie gave up smoking of her own accord. It is a pattern that I observe time and again; the moment we give up trying to change our partner – and accept him or her, warts and all – is the moment our partner becomes ready to change.

If you're thinking of offering the gift of acceptance, tell your partner that 'I would still like you to . . . [fill in the gap] but I realise that it's counterproductive to pressurise. So I'm going to stop dropping hints or trying to apply subtle pressure. It doesn't mean that I don't still want you to . . . but it's up to you.' It will take patience and persistence and you will have to bite your tongue occasionally. If you find yourself slipping, remember the Serenity Prayer attributed to American theologian Reinhold Niebuhr (1892–1971) and frequently used by Alcoholics Anonymous:

God, grant me the serenity
To accept the things I cannot change,
The courage to change the things that I can,
And the wisdom to know the difference.

WHAT I APPRECIATE ABOUT MY PARTNER

Rather than worrying about what you don't have, think about what you do. Put down as many examples of what you appreciate about your partner as possible. Don't overlook the tasks that are so everyday that they have become almost invisible – like filling up the car with petrol, putting out the recycling or buying toilet paper.

On an average weekday, my partner does the following for me:

....
....
....

On an average weekend, my partner does the following for me:

....
....
....

I admire the following qualities in my partner:

....
....
....

Go Beyond Cynicism

For more and more people, the standard default position is cynicism. In many ways, this is not surprising. We live in an increasingly individual-istic society – where everybody is encouraged to ask: 'What's in it for me?' Celebrities and poli-ticians are always being uncovered for saying one thing and doing another. On an average day, we see more than 3,500 brand images and are bombarded with messages that this or that product will bring us fulfilment and happiness. No wonder it is not just political interviewers who are asking themselves: 'Why is this lying bastard lying to me?'

However, for a relationship to flourish it is important to go beyond the cynicism of 'All men are after just one thing' and 'A clever woman knows how to get her own way', or 'I'll scratch your back, if you'll scratch mine.' Instead of expecting the worst, we need to move beyond gender stereotyping and look for the best in our partner. Rather than listening to the cynical back-ground music of newspapers and television – and the cynical voice in our own head claiming 'They would say that' – we need to embrace hope, compassion and, in particular, generosity.

Why is generosity so important? Instead of waiting passively for our partner to make the first move, or offer some sign of encouragement, we need to take control and act ourselves. It might take a generous spirit to give – with no strings attached and no expectation of a return. However, when someone finds that level of generosity, it can completely turn a relationship round.

When Joanne was being courted by Sebastian, he seemed a great romantic. He'd written the most amazing letters and driven through the night to be with her. But after the wedding everything changed. 'He wasn't telling me that he loved me any more and he was spending more and more time in the garage on his bikes or with his collection of antique pocket watches, so he had no time for me at all,' said Joanne. 'I would want to talk about it and he couldn't understand that I was upset. He would take everything I said literally and tell me "If you're not happy, it was a big mistake and we'll just get divorced." But I just wanted to know what was wrong.' The low point was a weekend break in Bath. 'We stood on a bridge and discussed financially what we'd do if we got divorced. Although there was a lot of equity in the house, he was completely and utterly prepared to give it all to me. No questions. I looked at him and thought: You do love me, but there's something weird about you.'

As it turned out, Sebastian had Asperger's Syndrome – a type of autism characterised by an inability to read body language, poor social skills, and a narrow, obsessive range of interests. However, I tell the story because Sebastian's generosity broke through their crisis and the couple are still happily married ten years later. Even if your relationship is ticking along reasonably happily, being generous and making the first move – without worrying who is giving the most – can start a revolution.

Compassion is useful because it helps us cross over any gender differences and value our partner's take on important issues. For example, I counsel many couples who have different interpretations of what constitutes intimacy. 'I'm not asking for much,' said Tina, thirty-seven, 'just not to be taken for granted, to be told I love you without having to ask and those little gestures that show he cares.' Her husband, Dieter, seemed to want the polar opposite: 'But I want an easy, comfortable relationship where I feel secure enough to take love for granted and where I don't have to be always checking how it is going.' They had been dismissing each other's needs by complaining 'He's a typical man' or 'I just don't understand women'. However, when they were compassionate and found a way through the cynicism, they each discovered that their particular form of intimacy did not exclude their partner's. Tina admitted: 'I love the simple warmth of lying next to Dieter and hearing his companionable heartbeat.' And Dieter accepted: 'I like feedback and reassurance too.'

Finally, going beyond cynicism allows hope to flourish. This is ultimately the most important ingredient for a successful relationship. During the dark moments, we need hope that things will get better. It also helps us believe that love is something more than a business deal where you agree to one set of things and your partner agrees to another.

THE MOST IMPORTANT EXERCISE OF ALL

It is hard to be generous, compassionate and hold on to hope. Sometimes making the first move is such a giant leap of faith that I reassure my clients and say: Just experiment.

- Rather than making a commitment to do something for ever, just experiment – once or twice or maybe for a week.
- At the end of your short time-frame, reassess your progress.
- If you are generous, compassionate and enter the experiment full of hope, I guarantee that things will not be worse. Most likely, they will be a whole lot better.
- Finally, look back through the book and think about the exercises or ideas that you would like to adopt but which seemed too hard. Why not experiment and try them for a week too?

I did this exercise with Janet, forty-eight, whose husband had left, asking for 'time to sort myself out'. Rather than taking the heat off their problems, it had made things worse and the couple would fire angry texts back and forth. I asked Janet to experiment and find out what would happen if she sent only nice texts for a week – after all, she wanted to repair their relationship and for her husband to return home.

Janet returned a week later, all smiles. Her husband had sent a text full of swear words and recriminations about the amount of money she had spent decorating the house. However, she had

kept her calm and had texted back: 'I understand that you're angry but painting is the only
thing that's kept me sane. I miss you. Janet.'
When he bought their daughter a mobile phone,
even though they had previously agreed that she
wasn't old enough, Janet bit her tongue and said
nothing. 'How has the experiment gone?' I asked.
'It took quite a bit of self-restraint but I didn't
wind myself up composing nasty texts. Better still,
I didn't have to cope with all his angry replies. So
not only have we been getting on better, but I've
also felt better in myself.'

Find a Better Understanding of Love

When couples who have grown and changed
look back at their journey, remember the knowledge acquired and the new skills learned, they
find a lasting belief in themselves. So what is this
knowledge?

- Love is effort. In a good relationship, both
  partners regularly and routinely attend to each
  other's needs – no matter how they feel. This
  extra mile is often what is most appreciated.

- Love is about both giving *and* receiving. In a good relationship, both partners make certain they find the joy in both halves of the equation.
- Love is courage. In a good relationship, both partners share their vulnerabilities as well as their strengths and do not close themselves off, shut down or take the easy option.
- Love is rewarding. In a good relationship, both partners support each other and help each other grow.
- Love is most appreciated when a couple thought it was lost for ever, but have subsequently found a way back to each other again.

What about the skills learned?

- To be honest with oneself.
- To be honest with your partner.
- To be up-front about differences, rather than ignoring or hiding them away.
- To negotiate better.
- To find a genuine compromise, rather than one partner just backing down or steam-rollering over the other.

Summing Up

There are six helpful habits which build on each other and will ensure your relationship continues to grow and flourish. If you 'understand the pattern' of disputes with your partner, you will move beyond blaming each other. This will make it easier to 'have fun together' and to discover a 'third way' round difficult arguments. By 'accepting what you can't change' and 'going beyond cynicism', you will 'find a better understanding of love'.

IN A NUTSHELL:

- Take a cynical thought and replace it with a kinder one.
- Tolerating and forgiving your partner's failings makes it easier to accept your own.
- Love is about giving and receiving.

FINAL NUTSHELLS

1. Stop What Doesn't Work

We are more likely to be influenced by people whom we like. So creating a contented atmosphere will make you that little bit more persuasive.

- Look at the ways you currently try and get your own way: are they working or do they just get your partner's back up?
- Lower the temperature by stopping failed strategies such as lecturing, sarcasm, demanding, nagging and inducing guilt. Even milder strategies – for example, placating and dropping hints – can annoy your partner and make him or her irritable or sarcastic.
- Check that your request is fair.

Checkpoint: Stop communicating all the negatives and start thinking about the positives. What one small thing did you appreciate about your partner today? It might be getting up in the middle of the night to find the cough medicine, buying that really good cut of meat or just phoning to say hello. Make the commitment to communicate one positive every day; you could text or email it or maybe just tell your partner.

2. Do Less

Change is frightening and sets up our fight or flight response.

- If your partner strongly disagrees with your suggestion, he or she will be too busy fighting it to truly listen.
- If your partner flees and buries him- or herself in some all-consuming task, he or she is not listening either.
- No attention = No communication = No result.
- Therefore, instead of going for big changes, ask small questions, solve small problems

and make small incremental changes to your relationship.

- Little changes not only build to have a big effect, but also one success breeds another. So although there is a slow start, improvements come faster and faster.

Checkpoint: Ask your friends: What one small thing does your partner do that makes you happy? Every time they give you something concrete – he sends a postcard even if he's only away for one night – write it down and use it for inspiration for small changes in your own relationship.

3. Think Smarter

Seemingly insignificant details can have a major impact on our behaviour. At first sight, the idea that everything matters might seem paralysing, but it is also empowering.

- We can easily get stuck in a rut where we automatically do the same things.
- A small push in the right direction, a nudge, can break this inertia and set up good habits.

- Nudges work best for situations that happen frequently, especially where previously there has been little or no discussion about how to divide tasks and when short-term benefits (like sitting down and having a drink) outweigh long-term ones (like doing the ironing and having a clean shirt for the morning).
- It counts as a nudge only when your partner is still free to choose.

Checkpoint: Picture what you want in detail. Instead of general unfocused goals like to be 'happy' or 'get on', flesh out the details. Imagine that you could climb into a time machine and go forward three months. By this point, you will have digested all the thoughts in this book and begun to transfer them into your everyday life. Look around this near future: What sort of things would the two of you be doing? How would life be different? Imagine that you could step off the time machine and wander around your new life. How do the two of you relate to each other? Finally, coming back to today: What specific goals would you like to set?

4. Carrots Rather Than Sticks

Although it requires two people to change a relationship, one partner can always take the lead.

- You need five positives to outweigh one negative.
- So why not experiment with focusing entirely on the positive?
- Discuss what works in your relationship and what resources you can use to improve your relationship.
- Being positive will make it easier to recruit your partner and gain his or her cooperation.

Checkpoint: When you're considering asking your partner a question, in order to move your relationship forward, give it the 'genuine test'. By this I mean is it an open question (how, what, which) and not pointing towards your preferred option? The best-framed questions are ones to which you genuinely don't know the answer but want your partner's help to figure it out. For example: 'What should we do with our retirement?' or 'How do we keep our love life fresh?'

5. Change Your Behaviour

When a relationship needs improving, it is much easier to complain about our partner's contribution to the problems than to look at our own.

- How has *your* behaviour contributed to the problem? What could you learn from your partner? How could you become more of a team? Answering these questions will help you move towards the middle of an issue and become more balanced.
- Knowing which part of your personality is in play – Parent, Adult or Child – and how that affects the response of your partner is key to improving communication.
- 'People are OK.' Learning to like yourself and remembering your partner's good qualities can transform your relationship.
- Understand the link between your interpretation of events and your feelings, and question any negative automatic thoughts, assumptions and beliefs.

Checkpoint: In a successful relationship, partners not only look after each other but also themselves. Unfortunately, some people focus all their care on their partner – hoping he or she will return the favour. In the meantime, they become emotionally exhausted and either sacrifice their needs (and become a people-pleaser) or become resentful (and become a serial complainer). So what have you done lately to nurture yourself? What would you like to do? How could your partner help facilitate this activity – perhaps by looking after your children?

6. Coming Back From Crisis Point

You have to believe that your relationship will work and act lovingly towards your partner.

- Don't be panicked into short-term coping mechanisms that actually make the relationship worse.
- Acknowledge the issues, take your share of the responsibility and listen – truly listen – to your partner.
- Once problems are out in the open, they can finally be addressed.
- Slow and steady progress, underpinned by patience and tenacity, will save the day.

Checkpoint: When we are stressed, we find it hard to take in what our partner is saying. Even under the best circumstances, we take in only 46 per cent of what we're told and therefore need to have it repeated. So follow this golden rule for communicating something important: say it and then repeat what you have said.

7. No Turning Back

If you keep on doing what you've always done, you'll keep on getting the same results, so make a commitment to change.

- Create good habits rather than making a special effort.
- Accepting your partner's foibles and failings as 'facts of life' rather than 'problems to be solved' will allow your partner to make an important internal shift.
- Once your partner does not feel judged, he or she can look at their behaviour through new eyes and be open to change.
- Cynicism is one of the greatest threats to relationships today. When your friends or work colleagues bond by moaning about their partner's failings,

don't join in. These discussions just pump up our dissatisfaction and unhappiness.

Checkpoint: Make certain your strategies for persuading your partner are SMART. By this I mean:

Specific
Measurable
Achievable
Realistic
Timed (i.e., there is a date for completion)

FINAL NUTSHELL:

- Ask for what you need in an open and direct manner. Your partner is more likely to say 'yes' if he or she understands what you want.
- Enjoy touching your partner – for example: in the small of the back when guiding her through the door or rubbing his shoulders while you're watching television together. Better cooperation comes from making your partner feel valued.
- When your partner talks, give her or him your full attention. Good communication comes from understanding their viewpoint.

A Note on the Author

Andrew G. Marshall is a marital therapist and the author of *I Love You But I'm Not In Love With You: Seven Steps to Saving Your Relationship*, *The Single Trap: The Two-step Guide to Escaping It and Finding Lasting Love* and *How Can I Ever Trust You Again?: Infidelity: From Discovery to Recovery in Seven Steps*. He writes for *The Times*, the *Mail on Sunday*, the *Guardian*, *Psychologies* and women's magazines around the world. His work has been translated into over fifteen languages. Andrew trained with RELATE and has a private practice offering counselling, workshops, training days and inspirational talks.

www.andrewgmarshall.com

THE SEVEN STEPS SERIES

ARE YOU RIGHT FOR ME?

Seven steps to getting clarity and commitment in your relationship

ISBN 9781408802625 · PAPERBACK · £6.99

∗

HELP YOUR PARTNER SAY 'YES'

Seven steps to achieving better cooperation and communication

ISBN 9781408802632 · PAPERBACK · £6.99

∗

LEARN TO LOVE YOURSELF ENOUGH

Seven steps to improving your self-esteem and your relationships

ISBN 9781408802618 · PAPERBACK · £6.99

∗

RESOLVE YOUR DIFFERENCES

Seven steps to coping with conflict in your relationship

ISBN 9781408802595 · PAPERBACK · £6.99

∗

BUILD A LIFE-LONG LOVE AFFAIR

Seven steps to revitalising your relationship

ISBN 9781408802557 · PAPERBACK · £6.99

∗

HEAL AND MOVE ON

Seven steps to recovering from a break-up

ISBN 9781408802601 · PAPERBACK · £6.99

ORDER YOUR COPY:

BY PHONE: +44 (0)1256 302 699;

BY EMAIL: DIRECT@MACMILLAN.CO.UK

ONLINE: WWW.BLOOMSBURY.COM/BOOKSHOP

WWW.BLOOMSBURY.COM

BLOOMSBURY